# PREHISTORIC ART AND ANCIENT
ART OF THE NEAR EAST

DISCOVERING ART SERIES

# Prehistoric Art and Ancient Art of the Near East

adapted by Ariane Ruskin

*Foreword by Howard Conant*
*New York University*

McGRAW-HILL BOOK COMPANY
*New York • San Francisco • Toronto*

Acknowledgment is hereby given to Purnell & Sons, Ltd., for the right to base this work on the text of the magazine series "Discovering Art," and to Fratelli Fabbri Editori for the right to make adaptations from the Italian text of *Capolavori Nei Secoli*.

PREHISTORIC ART AND ANCIENT ART OF THE NEAR EAST
Illustrations copyright © 1961–1964, 1971 by Fratelli Fabbri Editori, Milan, Italy. No part of this work may be reproduced without the permission of the publisher. All Rights Reserved. *Printed in Italy*.

Library of Congress Catalog Card Number: 72-154838

# FOREWORD

by Howard Conant,

*Professor and Chairman, Department of Art Education; and Head, Division of Creative Arts, New York University*

PREHISTORIC ART AND ART OF THE NEAR EAST is, in itself, a foreword—a foreword to the entire history of man, his culture, and his art. This volume introduces us to the basic life stimuli and functions which have engendered and shaped art forms since their inception, it also creates a presence, an atmosphere, in which the reader can almost feel the throbbing pulsation of prehistoric man's origins. And thanks to the more than 200 magnificently reproduced color illustrations, we can see for ourselves tangible proof of the astonishing artistic skill with which our very earliest predecessors were endowed. Indeed, in one place and at one time we are able to see clearly and thoughtfully compare works which, at the time of their creation were only dimly torch-lit, often inaccessable, and widely separated in time and place.

This volume traces man's creative efforts and describes in fascinating detail the various cultural milieu and life styles through which he passed from the time of the Upper Paleolithic period through the ancient Egyptian and Mesopotamian civilizations. It thus provides us with essential background information for the multitude of art periods and styles described in other volumes in this series.

But by far, the most important and probably unique feature of this book is what it tells us about the nature of art. Quite unlike the "art as decoration" or "art as museum objects" notions which have evolved in recent centuries, art in prehistoric and ancient times was so much a part of man's everyday life that it was not even known as "art." PREHISTORIC ART AND ANCIENT ART OF THE NEAR EAST, together with its companion volumes in the Discovering Art Series, belongs in every home and school library.

# CONTENTS

WHEN WE SPEAK of the *Paleolithic Era,* we are using an expression derived from Greek meaning, literally, Old Stone Age. A *Stone Age* culture is one in which man uses tools made of carefully chipped and fashioned stone. The Old Stone Age in Europe was the period we generally think of when we use the term *cave man,* and all of us have some idea of the life of this cave man, who dressed in animal pelts and hunted for his food, who had little notion of how to build a house and none of how to grow crops. It is amazing to us, then, that the one occupation, besides hunter, in which the cave man engaged that is still familiar to us now, was that of *artist.* The profession of artist was among the first for which an individual was singled out from his fellows and trained.

It was during the last part of the Old Stone Age, the Upper Paleolithic period, that art as we know it today came into existence. The man of the earlier Old Stone Age had been the heavy-browed Neanderthal man (whose remains were first discovered at Neanderthal in Germany), with his receding jaw and brain somewhat smaller than that of modern man. Now a new species of man, tall and upright, with a high forehead and a larger brain, appeared. He is called by archeologists *Neoanthropic man,* literally, *new man.*

This *new man* came into Europe at a time when the last great ice cap that had held Europe in its grip throughout much of the Old Stone Age was receding. But it receded slowly. The Ice Age remained upon the European continent throughout the Old Stone Age, and men lived within view of the great glaciers that covered much of the northern part of the continent. Temperatures were somewhat colder than they are in most of Europe today, and animals we associate now with the forests of the far north—herds of reindeer, the stag, the bison, the Arctic fox, and the brown bear—roamed the tundra of southern France and Spain. There were wild horses and cattle, too, as well as great beasts now extinct—the mammoth and the woolly rhinoceros.

These were the prey of man, who lived, warmed by an open fire, in caves or shelters dug in the earth, and roofed with hides supported on branches or tusks and sometimes covered with heaped-up earth. He attacked them with his own carefully fashioned spears and other weapons, and when he returned with a kill, he cleverly put every bit of the carcass to use. The skin was used for warmth and shelter, the flesh for food, and the bone and tusk for tools. Flint, easily chipped and shaped, was also used for tools, and these tools became more finely worked and more complicated. In addition to many cleverly designed cutting instruments, man had devised the fine-eyed needle by the end of the Old Stone Age. He seems to have been concerned with matters other than sheer brute survival. He decorated his body with jewelry, sometimes made of sea shells that must have been brought over great distances, and he had thought of an afterlife—his dead were buried with ceremony. Above all, he devoted considerable effort to the beautification of the objects with which he lived and to the creation of what we think of even today as art: sculpture and painting.

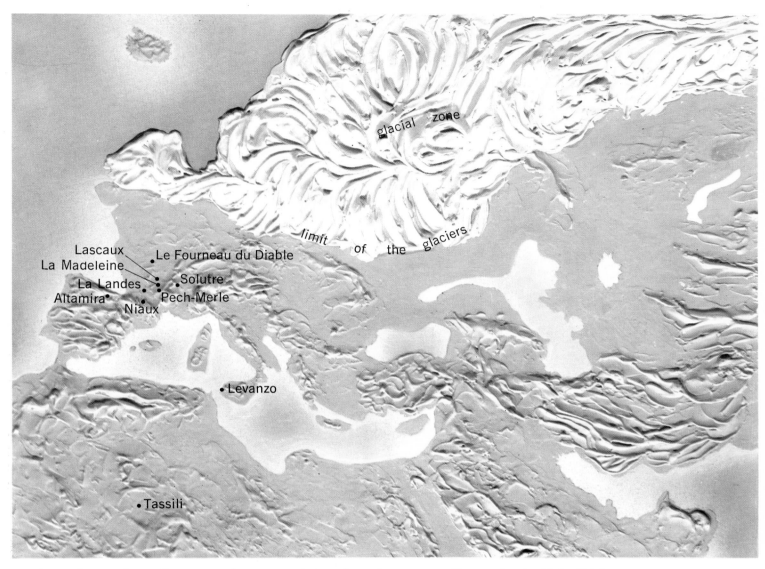

I-1. Areas in southern Europe and western Asia where important discoveries in Paleolithic art have been made.

The Upper Paleolithic period lasted from about 40,000 to 10,000 B.C., a full 30,000 years, almost six times the period that separates us from the very earliest pyramids of Egypt (Plate I-1). Within this long span artistic activity has been divided into three periods, each named after a culture which reigned during that era in Europe. By *culture* we mean the manner of making, decorating, and using artifacts which appears to have been developed by a group and spread throughout a specific area. These three periods are the Aurignacian (roughly 30,000 to 20,000 B.C.), the Solutrian (roughly 20,000 to 15,000 B.C.), and the Magdalenian (15,000 to 10,000 B.C.), named after three places concentrated in the region of the Pyrenees and southwestern France, where the richest deposits of remains have been found. The Aurignacian is named after the French district of Aurignac, the Solutrian after the area of Solutré, and the Magdalenian after the famous caves of La Madeleine. It is the first and last of these cultures that interest us most, for Solutrian man seems to have been an invader from eastern Europe who brought new tools but no art with him, and wherever he did not penetrate, Aurignacian culture seems to have developed directly into Magdalenian.

Among the earliest examples of Paleolithic art are tiny figures of women carved either from stone or from mammoth ivory, or sometimes molded in clay and ash carefully. They have been found in a wide area extending from France and Italy to as far as Siberia. At the end of the last century an antique dealer found a whole col-

I-3. Ivory female statuette, found in Landes, France.

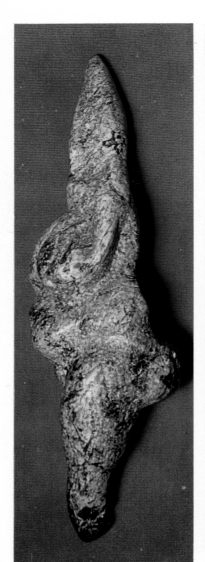

I-2. **Venus of Savignano, from near the river Panaro in northern Italy.**

I-4. **Soapstone female figurine, from Balzi Rossi caves, Ventimiglia, Italy.**

lection of these little female statuettes in the Balzi Rossi caves at Ventimiglia in Italy.

These statuettes, flatteringly called Venuses by archeologists, may not be forms of beauty by modern standards. They are exaggerated little figures, stressing woman's reproductive role. They show her with heavy breasts, a protruding belly, and wide hips. Little else seems to matter: the arms are either unfinished, or meager appendages extended across the figure's breasts, the legs taper to a footless nothing, and the heads are mere knobs (Plates I-2, I-3, I-4, and I-5). The figures are not all the same, however. They vary, and some have quite unusual features. One soapstone statuette from the Balzi Rossi shows greater realism than the others, and we sense that this is the torso of a real woman (Plate I-6). The headless statue of the Venus of Sireuil (Plate I-7), found near a quarry in Dordogne, is strikingly different from other prehistoric figures in its tense twisting back position. The Venus of Willendorf sports an elaborate hair style which almost covers her face (Plate I-8). Such detail is unusual. Few of the figures of women have any indication of facial features, and few appear to be wearing a garment or girdle. The smallness of their size (the Venus of Willendorf is just 4½ inches long) and the crudeness of the sculptor's tools partly account for this.

But detail was unimportant. Above all, these figurines represented what was most important to primitive man: fertility and the perpetuation of the race. It seems most probable that they were what we call *cult* or religious objects used in some ritual. Women were entrusted with the power of carrying on the race, and this function appeared so important and mysterious to early men that they perhaps felt that images of women could fulfill a magical or religious purpose, that of encouraging fertility.

I-6. **Soapstone female figurine, from Balzi Rossi caves, Ventimiglia, Italy.**

I-5. **Soapstone female figurine, from Balzi Rossi caves, Ventimiglia, Italy.**

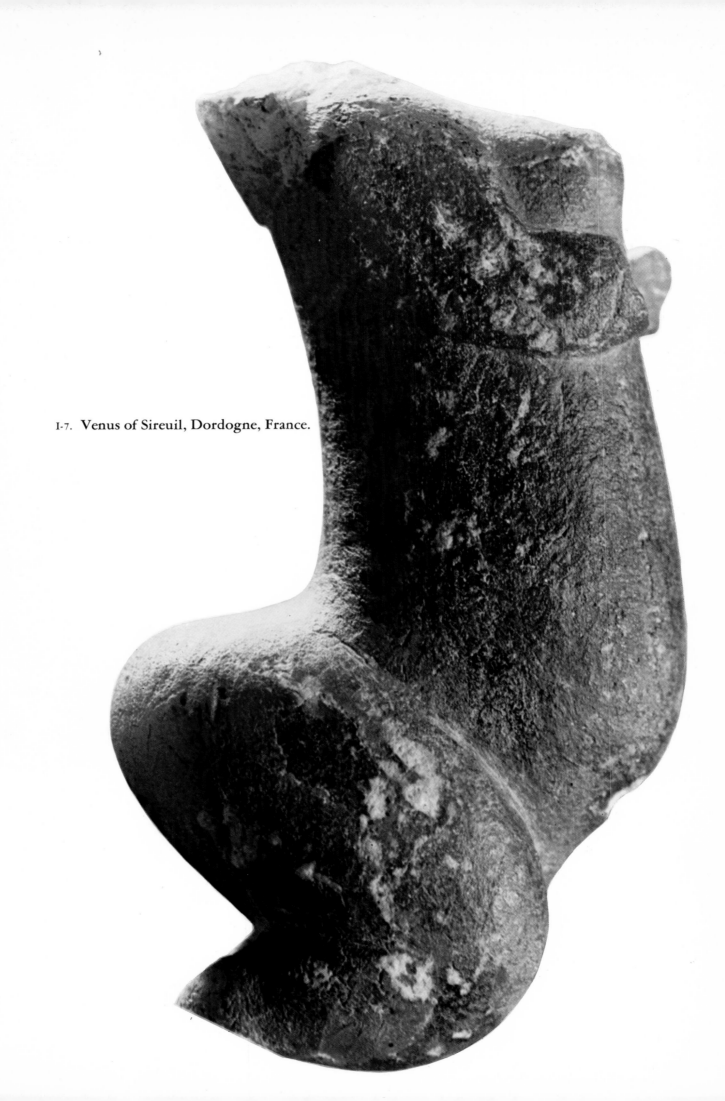

I-7. Venus of Sireuil, Dordogne, France.

bols representing an ideal, not a specific individual. But there is some evidence that primitive artists went further, that they sometimes attempted to portray, as best they could, recognizable individuals. An astonishing example is the finely carved female head found at Landes in France (Plate I-9).

I-9. Female head, from Landes, France.

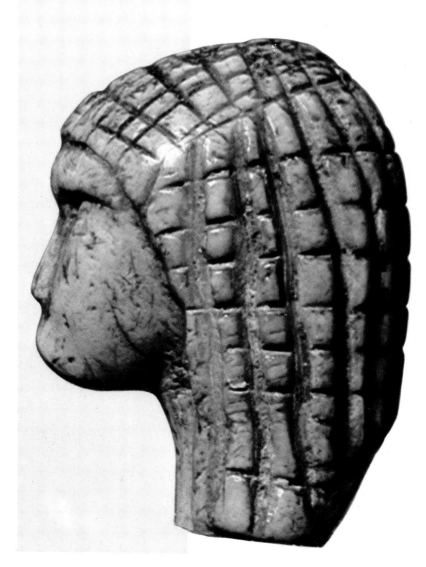

To modern tastes, these figures would appear unnecessarily obese. This, too, may have been symbolic. To primitive man, fat represented a plentiful food supply and the opposite of starvation. And so these strange little figures, perhaps ugly to our eyes, represented to our ancestors everything that was desirable—food and children, the continuation of the race.

As we have said, these figures were sym-

I-10. **Negroid head, from Balzi Rossi caves, Ventimiglia, Italy.**

With its elaborate coiffure it is surely a portrait of some young girl who lived tens of thousands of years ago. Equally amazing is the Negroid head from Balzi Rossi (Plate I-10). This head, in spite of its small size, shows a definitely Negroid face. It is not mere coincidence, since two skeletons of Negro type have been found at Balzi Rossi. This may perhaps be explained by the fact that Spain was still joined to Africa during this period.

But such examples of the cave artist's close observation of individual types when depicting human beings are rare. Strangely, he seems to have reserved this skill for his portrayal of animals, and these he painted and sculpted with an artistry and beauty that have rarely been surpassed.

The Venuses of Balzi Rossi and the many like them throughout Europe are art in the sense that they are among the earliest examples of man's effort to reproduce with his own hands what he saw in the world around him. These, too, are the first examples of sculpture in the round—three-dimensional art. But in his attempt to portray animals, sketching them with in-cised lines on rock surfaces, painting them or sculpting them, he attempted to convey what we recognize even today as the beauty in nature. For reasons that we shall see, the artist experimented constantly in order to depict his subjects more and more realistically, in every pose of rest or motion in which the hunter saw them. And yet there is reason to believe that the same artists, or at least men of the same culture, created both the plump and almost lifeless Venuses and the amazingly vivid animals. There are several works that link the two. The Venus of Laussel, a low relief from Dordogne, shows a woman holding a buffalo's horn (Plate I-11), and at Angles-sur-l'Anglin, three lifesized female figures of the Magdalenian times have been found carved in relief in a cliff face, along with the figures of bison, ibex, and horse.

Primitive man may have noticed that some stone or rock suggested the shape of some other object, such as the human body, and this may have been the origin of his attempts at sculpture in the round. The rendering of three-dimensional images on the flat surface of a cave wall is a more subtle idea, however. There is evidence, though, that early man might have noticed some scratches made by animals' claws on a flat surface, which suggested in two dimensions objects with which he was familiar. In any case, it was a technique which he developed with all the skill of the most advanced mind of any living creature, and the results of his efforts, the great cave paintings of late Paleolithic animal life, hold us in awe today for their beauty, realism, and vitality.

The cave paintings were not so widely distributed as the little female fertility figures. As we have seen, the best known are to be found for the most part in the area of southwestern France and the Pyrenees.

Needless to say, until the last century their very existence was undreamed of. When, in 1868, the Spanish archeologist Don Marcelino S. de Santuola first entered the great cave of Altamira, he failed to see certain black markings on the wall. Some years later his daughter was the first to notice that, upon close inspection, the walls and ceilings of the cave were covered with animal paintings. It was many years still before these were accepted as the work of man's primeval, cave-dwelling ancestor. Probably the most dramatic tale of discovery is that of four boys in France who, in 1940, went looking for a lost dog and literally fell into the cave of Lascaux.

As we have said, Paleolithic man's great genius was for painting animals. Apart from the need to perpetuate himself and his species, his all-important interest and concern was hunting, on which his whole existence depended. And the hunters of western Europe during the last Ice Age evolved the most brilliant culture ever created by hunters and food gatherers in any part of the world. It is natural, then, that the favored theme of prehistoric art should be animals, and as we shall see, the painting of animals was closely involved with the art of hunting itself. In painting and sculpture, beasts are represented with marvelous accuracy and sympathy. The much rarer representations of human beings in the company of animals are stylized like the fertility Venuses. In this case they are mere stick figures, often sporting an animal mask rather like those worn by witch doctors in parts of Africa today. This may have been due not so much to inability on the part of the artist, as to an unwillingness to make likenesses of living persons, a reluctance often found among primitive peoples.

The artists of the cave paintings were gifted men and specialized craftsmen. The

I-11. **Venus of Laussel, from Dordogne, France.**

boldness and mastery of their pictures could not have been acquired without training and practice. In fact, from such evidence as we have, it would seem that their study and practice of art was remarkably like today's. Like the great masters of the Renaissance and other periods, cave artists seem to have tried out their skill by experimenting with rough sketches before setting to work on a larger ground. At Altamira, for instance, pieces of bone engraved with heads of hinds were found in a stratum which was early Magdalenian. Similar heads, treated in an identical style, are drawn on the cave walls. Again, in 1925, a tiny engraving of a bison with a hump behind his head was found on a sliver of limestone in a mid-Magdalenian stratum in a rock shelter. This was the sketch for a painting of the same peculiar looking animal in the famous cave of Font-de-Gaume 200 miles away, which had been discovered twenty-four years earlier. Stone slivers and pebbles found at Limeuil in the Dordogne suggest that the cave might actually have been an artist's studio. In some sketches, the figures are repeated, both well and poorly drawn, as if by a master and pupil, and some even show corrections.

The painters' materials and equipment were amazingly varied and showed great ingenuity. Different kinds of ocher, found in deposits in the caves themselves, supplied browns, reds, and yellows. Blacks were made from manganese earth, some form of iron oxide, charcoal, and lampblack from lamps burning animal fat. Rare white marl was used to obtain white. These colors may have been mixed with animal fat, vegetable oil, albumen, or possibly blood to bind them, and they have withstood the test of many millennia remarkably well. In some caves, sealed from the air by landslides, they are as fresh as the day they were applied. There is some slight evidence of the existence of blue pigments but none of green. This may be because the cave artist painted animals, never landscapes. It may also be that such pigments existed but have faded and are no longer to be seen.

Bowls have been discovered in the caves in which these pigments were reduced to powder and then made into paste. The artist even seems to have used tubes of bone in which to keep his powdered colors, and bone palettes on which to mix them. The paints were applied with fingers at first, and later with brushes. These were made of chewed pieces of wood or a pad of fur or a bunch of feathers for daubing, or of hair for fine work. Earth crayons, all carefully pointed, have been found, and some color seems to have been sprayed on the wall surface with a blowpipe.

The technique of the cave painter did not appear all at once, but like all schools of art, developed slowly, step by step, over a long period of time. For this reason it is very important that we should be able to date cave paintings correctly, and this is sometimes difficult because the works of one age are often painted directly over those of another.

The dates of many cave paintings and engravings of the Upper Paleolithic Age can be determined by a careful examination of archeological levels. In some caverns the pictures first came to light when the cave-fillings, consisting of strata laid down in the Ice Age, were removed. Obviously these pictures were older than the layers of earth and debris which had covered them, and which could be identified and dated by geologists and archeologists. Besides, many small objects, like sticks of reindeer bone with holes bored through them, stones and pieces of horn and ivory, pendants and spear-throwers and concave stones which served as lamps, have been found in the cave strata. Their age can often be determined by the type of craftsmanship with which they were made, and this helps to indicate the age of the paintings in the same cave.

During the past ten years it has been possible to determine roughly, up to an age of 40,000 years, the antiquity of any object of organic origin through the Carbon-14 or radio-carbon count. All living things absorb a radioactive isotope of Carbon-14 while they are alive, and after death the Carbon-14 decays at the same regular rate under all circumstances. So objects made from tusk and bone, which would have perished in the open air but have been preserved in the depths of caves, provide valuable clues to the age of other finds in the same layer.

Among the earliest of all cave paintings are hands stenciled in red, brown, black, or violet, like those in the caves of Pech-Merle (Plate I-12). Curiously enough, this method of reproducing the hand on a flat surface by simply outlining one's own hand, something children learn in kindergarten, was the first technique man seems to have worked out for himself. He made the outlines by blowing ocher from his mouth over a hand laid flat on a rock and these stencils belong to the Aurignacian period.

After hand paintings come line drawings in yellow, red, and sometimes black, like those of Pech-Merle and Cougnac. Here the pictures consist entirely of outline, and there is no sense of depth or perspective. At first, horns are shown frontally, although the figures are in profile, and only one pair of legs on one side is depicted. In later drawings the second pair appears. There is little or no action. And yet so telling and powerful is the artist's line, even at this early stage, that his figures seem full of life. The mammoths, their ground-sweeping coats drawn with just a few swift vertical lines, their faces completely buried in their long woolly manes, possess an almost comical charm (Plates I-13 and I-14). There is no interior shading, but lines soon begin to vary between thick and thin. In the painting of horses we find at Pech-Merle (Plate I-15), the animals' bodies are covered with rough dots, and the heavy black line with which they are drawn has been thickened to cover the entire area of their necks. It is interesting that among the great elks with branching antlers, the deer, and the ibexes we find painted at Cougnac, there

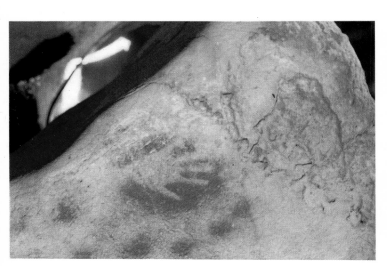

I-12. **Impression of a hand, from the cave of Pech-Merle, Dordogne, France.**

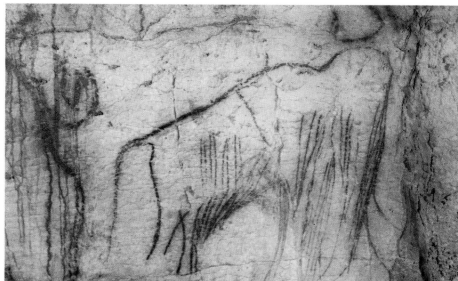

I-13. **Mammoths, from the cave of Pech-Merle, Dordogne, France.**

I-14. Mammoth, from the cave of Pech-Merle, Dordogne, France.

I-15. Two horses, from the cave of Pech-Merle, Dordogne, France.

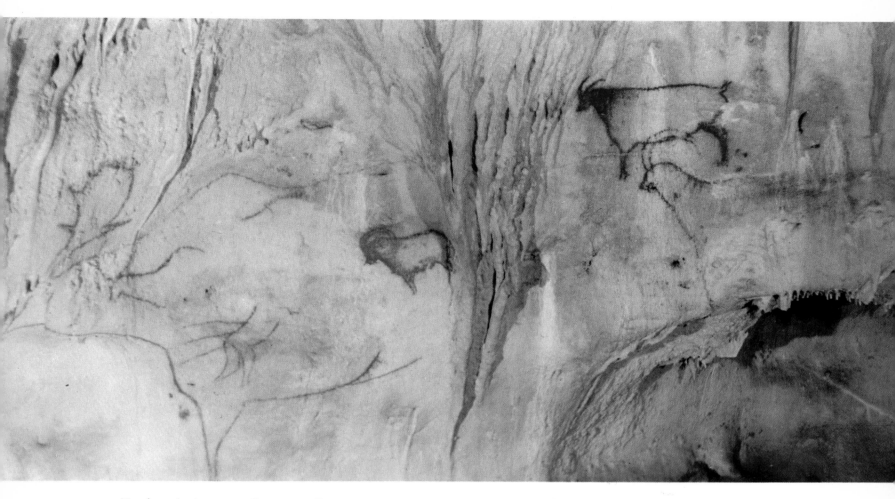

I-16. **Rock paintings, at Cougnac, France.**

are a few unfinished human figures, their bodies pierced with weapons (Plate I-16).

But the finest of all the cave paintings of the early or Aurignacian period are those found at Lascaux in France, the cave discovered by the small boys looking for their dog. In many sites, such as the great cave of Font-de-Gaume, the work of many periods is to be found superimposed, with figures of one period scratched over those of another. But here at Lascaux a large number of the paintings are of the same period and can be clearly seen against the white rock surface of the cave. They have remained especially clear because warm air, in which moisture condenses, does not penetrate to the depth of the cave.

The paintings of Lascaux are on a huge scale; some are 18 feet in length. A splendid variety of animals gallop and prance about the walls: oxen, bison, wild horses, bulls, deer and ibexes, a bear, a wolf, and a bird, as well as more extraordinary beasts—the rhinoceros and something that resembles a unicorn. Here the animals are in freer poses than we have seen before, and the complicated anatomy of their legs and joints seems almost perfectly understood. We can see in the powerful figure of a black bull (Plate I-17) that the artist has studied, too, the problems of depicting a pair of horns in a side view. He has carefully differentiated the foreshortened nearer horn. Above all, the figures on the walls

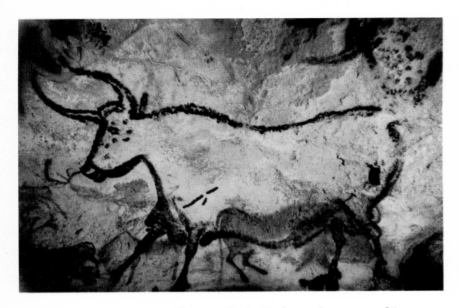

I-17. Figure of a bull, from the caves of Lascaux, Dordogne, France.

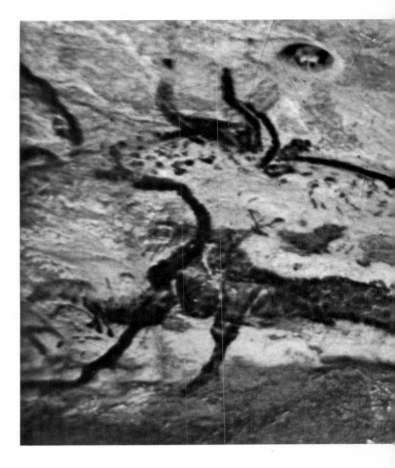

I-18. Leaping cow with a herd of horses, from the caves of Lascaux, Dordogne, France.

I-19. **Detail six bulls, from the caves of Lascaux, Dordogne, France.**

of Lascaux are full of action. The great bull paws the earth, and elsewhere on the wall a black cow literally leaps through the air (Plate I-18). Like all animal figures of the Old Stone Age, the cow is seen in profile, and yet so perfect is the artist's knowledge of anatomy that, while always in profile, the figure seems capable of any action. It is interesting that nearby we see a herd of horses of ancient type, short and stocky, with small heads and stumpy legs. We notice, too, in friezes like that of the six huge bulls (Plate I-19), that the sharp contour line of earlier work has softened and become more a part of the interior shape and modeling of the animal. Amazingly, each of these figures is about 5 yards long.

Among the great bulls in the main cave at Lascaux appears the head of one of the little deer we see in Plate I-20, reddish in color, with tall branching antlers as delicate as a cobweb. The deer are painted with a different technique: thin outlines are filled in with a red-ocher wash, which the artist applied by blowing pigment through a hollow bone. If it is carefully examined, the flat wash is found to be a series of blots forming a sort of dappled surface suggestive of soft fur. This technique of lively outline filled in with soft, flat color is typical of Lascaux, and we call this *polychrome* painting, that is, painting with more than one color. The muzzle of a bull appears in the left-hand corner of this plate, and if we look at Plate I-21, showing this bull along with

I-20. Herd of little deer, from the caves of Lascaux, Dordogne, France.

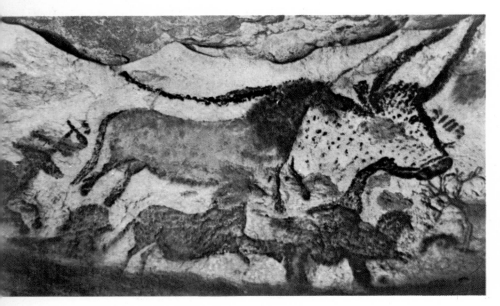

I-21. Bull, with herd of horses and deer on a smaller scale, from the caves of Lascaux, Dordogne, France.

galloping horses, we see that some figures are portrayed on a vastly different scale from others.

On one wall at Lascaux, we see a bison with its belly ripped open, a rhinoceros walking off to the left, and a human figure lying on its back. From this we may gather that a story has been told. The man or the rhinoceros may have killed the bison, and the bison or the rhinoceros may have in turn killed the man. But this sort of scene is unique.

One concept that the cave painter seemed to lack was any idea of what we consider an organized composition. He painted animals in friezes, that is, he painted strings of figures one after another. Or he would paint individual figures, and he might paint one on top of another for no easily visible reason. Moreover, as we have seen, he varied the scale of his animals enormously. All this suggests a purpose for his work other than mere decoration.

The art of the earlier caves is historically extraordinary, in fact almost incredible. And yet it was not until later in the Magdalenian period that cave art became what we recognize today as great art by any standard. In a way, the art of the Magdalenian period underwent its own development, beginning again with black and white sketches such as those to be seen in the caves at Niaux in France. Here we notice, in works like the bison pierced with arrows (Plate I-22), how a lively outline of free strokes and parallel hatching lines suggest the coarse fur and free, prancing movements of the animal. Again, in the sketch of a deer and the head of a horse, (Plate I-23) the line is remarkably telling. In the painting of an ibex or goat (Plate I-24), the artist has filled in the darkest part of the fur, giving a more finished impression. Most important, the buffaloes vigorously

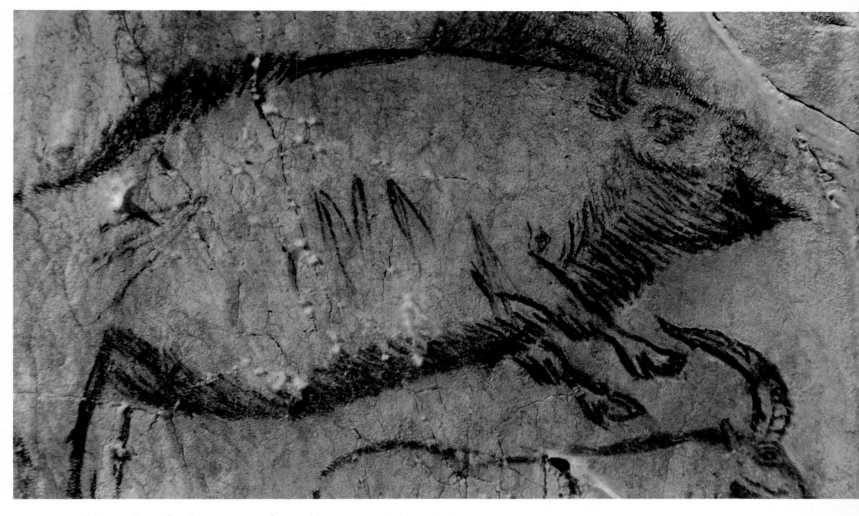

I-22. Bison pierced with arrows, from the caves at Niaux, France.

I-23. Paintings of a deer and the head of a horse, from the cave at Niaux, France.

I-24. Painting of an ibex, from the cave at Niaux, France.

I-25. **Sketch of buffaloes, from the cave at Niaux, France.**

sketched in black (Plate I-25) have a new grandeur and bulk. They are huge animals of mighty weight with massive shoulders.

This monumental bulkiness is especially apparent in the splendid animals of the great cave of Altamira in Spain. Stretched across 40 feet of ceiling near the entrance of this cave are the finest animal paintings in all prehistoric art. The splendid bull in Plate I-26, his great torso poised elegantly on his delicately drawn legs, has a superb magnificence. And here we see something we have not seen before in art. The round belly and powerful haunches of the beast are carefully shaped by a fine gradation of shading. In these *polychrome* paintings, not one or two but many colors are used to achieve an effect of modeled form. Moreover, the outline is hard where the bony structure is just under the surface of the skin, and soft where the eye would see only the furry pelt. This is all particularly clear at Altamira because the color, preserved in

the damp airlessness of the cave, is especially fresh and bright. The outline of the wild cow (Plate I-27) is as delicate and sensitive as any we have seen so far, and her body is carefully shadowed. Although there seems to be less motion here than at Lascaux, the animals appear wiry and tense, ready for action. The bison (Plate I-28) appears to be in a crouching position, with his legs pulled up under him. This may be because, like many of the animals at Altamira, the figure was painted to cover a natural lump-like projection on the ceiling itself. Cave artists did this wherever it was possible, in fact they seem to have deliberately shunned flat surfaces in favor of those that might give their figures some sculptural relief in order to achieve a heightened effect of realism.

Engraved sketches and actual relief sculpture developed along with the art of painting itself. The Venus of Laussel (Plate I-11) is the equivalent, in relief, of the

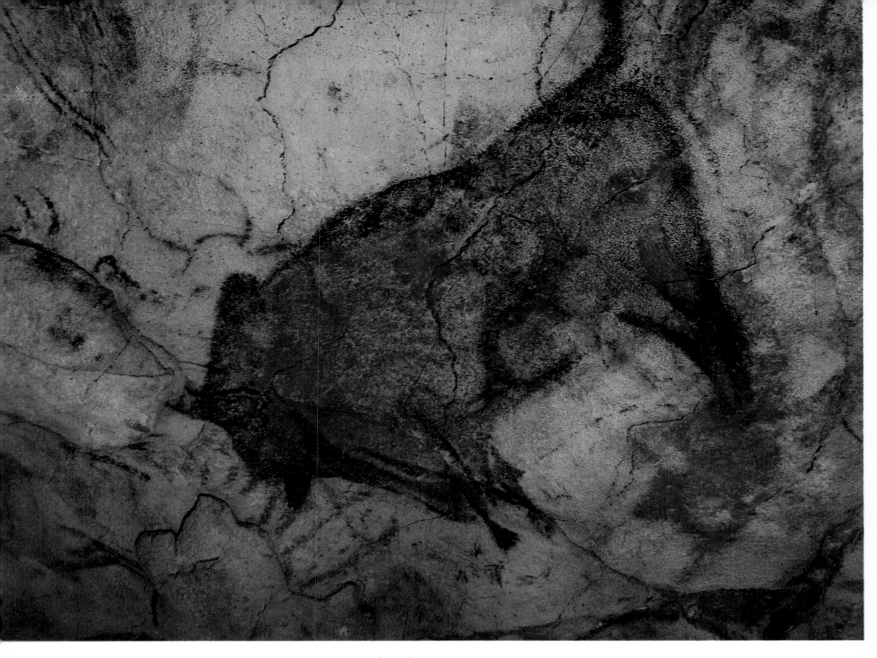

I-26. Bull, from the cave of Altamira, Santander, Spain.

I-27. Wild cow, from the cave of Altamira, Santander, Spain.

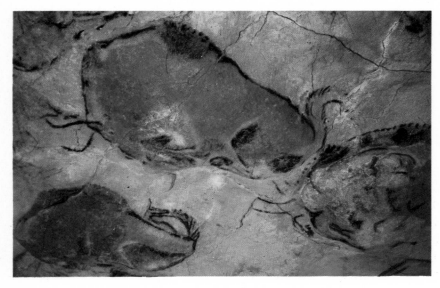

I-28. Crouching bison, from the cave of Altamira, Santander, Spain.

I-29. Hunting scene cut in slate, from a cave at Péchialet, France.

bulbous little fertility figures, while the bas-relief (low relief) of wild cattle from Le Fourneau du Diable in France Plate I-31 is worked with all the grace and all the knowledge of anatomy of the best of the animal cave paintings. Such reliefs were often in fact painted, and on some of them traces of color still remain. The relief we see in Plate I-32 from Le Roc de Sers seems to be a buffalo and appears to be sinking into the ground, wounded or dying. Some sketches were merely incised on soft stone surfaces, often lightly, like the hunting scene cut in slate which was found in a cave at Péchialet in southwest France (Plate I-29). Here we see a rare fight between a bear and two figures, one of them human. In the engraved sketch of a reindeer scratched in a surface of the caves of Les Combarelles in the Dordogne (Plate I-30), we see the graceful line of reindeer antlers we recognize from many Paleolithic paintings. (For some reason we do not know, although the reindeer was common in Europe throughout the Paleolithic period, which is sometimes called the "reindeer age," it appears far less often than other, rarer animals in prehistoric art.) The instruments the early engravers and relief sculptors used were tools with chisel-like edges or flint picks.

Small figures in the round, often carved of reindeer horn or ivory (Plate I-33), were common in the Magdalenian period, and these show a beauty and fine workmanship undreamed of by the sculptor of figures like the Venus of Willendorf (Plate I-8). The horse's head from Le Mas d'Azil (Plate I-34) is as excellent a piece of delicately carved realism as can be found at any period in art history. It is made of a projection on a deer's antler. Magdalenian sculptors often made use of the widest part of the antlers so as to make the most of branching horns. Another piece, a charming crouch-

I-30. Reindeer carved on rock in the caves of Les Combarelles, Dordogne, France.

I-31. Relief of wild cattle, from the cave of Le Fourneau du Diable, Charente, France.

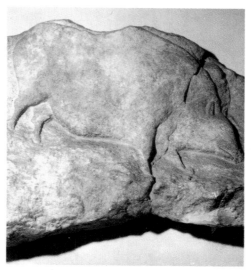

I-32. Relief of buffalo from Le Roc de Sers, Charente, France.

I-33. Engraving on a reindeer horn showing a stag following a gazelle, from the cave of La Madeleine, Dordogne, France.

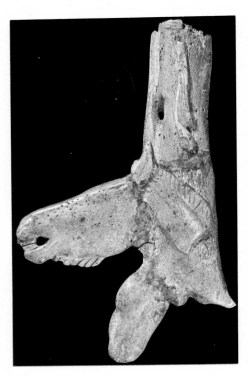

I-34. Carving of a horse's head, from Mas d'Azil, Ariège, France.

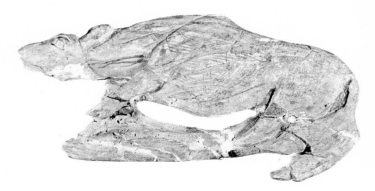

I-35. Crouching hyena carved in reindeer horn.

I-36. Female figure carved from a horse's tooth.

ing hyena (Plate I-35), is full of a tense life. Human representations of the period are few, and done with a much less sure hand. The tiny female figure in Plate I-36 is carved from a horse's tooth and is far less vivid and realistic than any of the animal figures. The artist seemed curiously to lack an idea of human proportions. The figure is far more primitive than that of the crouching hyena, although both are of the same period.

Many of these little ivory and bone figures are objects which prehistoric man used as tools and in his daily life. The headless ibex (Plate I-37) is carved on a sling. The sling or spear-thrower was one of the first "mechanical" weapons invented by prehistoric man and was used to hurl a pointed stick or spear, weighted with a piece of sharpened stone. The sling, which was often made of ivory or reindeer horn like this one, had a socket at one end into which the base of the spear was fitted. The bison

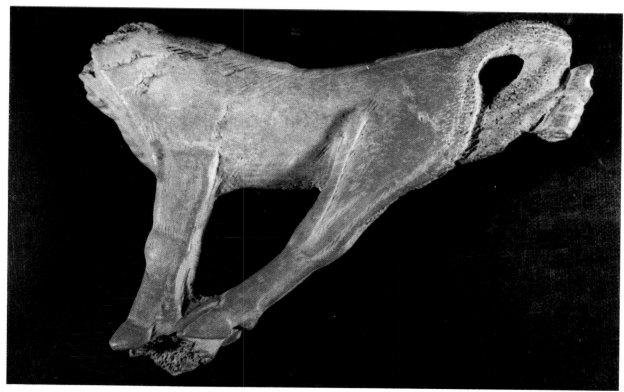

I-37. Ibex carved on a sling.

carved in reindeer horn from the cave of La Madeleine (Plate I-38), although only a few inches long, may also have formed the end of a sling. The sculptor has ingeniously carved the animal with its head turned back in a powerful movement, so as to fit it into his piece of horn. Another such bison (Plate I-39) is shown with his head lowered and neck outstretched, bellowing in a most realistic manner. This too may have decorated the end of a sling.

Paleolithic man, and the Magdalenians in particular, devoted great attention to adorning not only the surfaces of caves, but their personal possessions as well. They decorated their slings and spear-throwers with naturalistic carvings of horses, ibexes, goats, and other animals; and they even engraved the barbs and stems of the harpoons with which they speared salmon. Moreover the beauty, ingenuity, and craftsmanship they lavished on these objects suggest that making them must have been a

pleasure in itself. They showed the same love of artistic display in the jewelry with which they decked themselves. As early as the Aurignacian period (26,000–20,000), they wore necklaces; bracelets; headbands and kneebands; aprons of shells, animal teeth, and fish vertebrae; and even hairnets. The smooth, finely carved little ivory horse in Plate I-40 was probably a pendant or amulet worn to ward off evil spirits. All these small objects had their purpose, but what was the purpose of the great cave paintings and reliefs?

It is possible that the cave paintings were created merely to decorate man's habitation and to make his life pleasanter. But they have several inexplicable features which suggest some other purpose. We have already noticed that often one figure was painted or engraved right on top of another, and that the cave painter never developed a sense of composition. Moreover, the paintings are rarely to be found in caves that

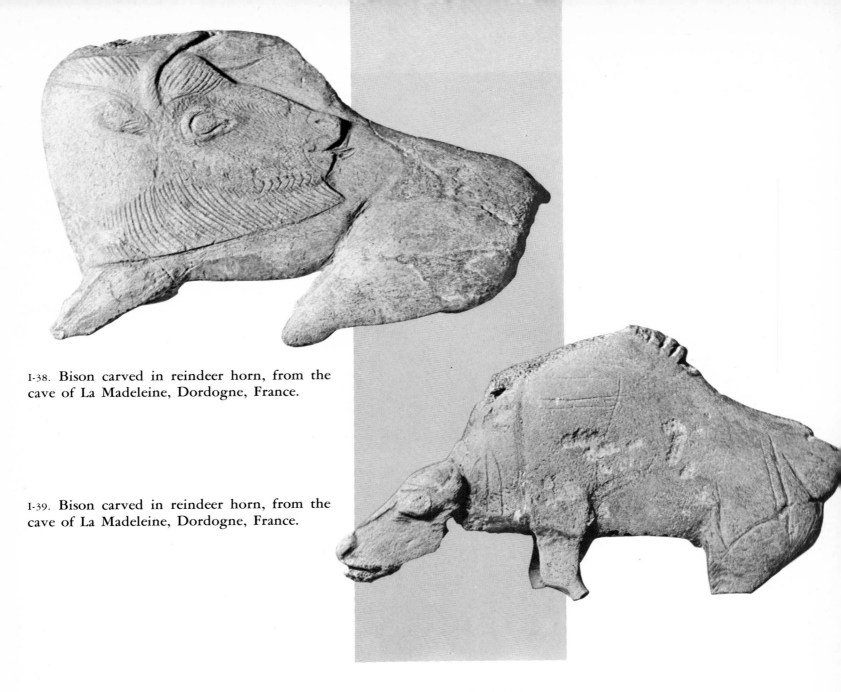

I-38. Bison carved in reindeer horn, from the cave of La Madeleine, Dordogne, France.

I-39. Bison carved in reindeer horn, from the cave of La Madeleine, Dordogne, France.

I-40. Ivory horse, which may have been used as a pendant or amulet.

were actually inhabited, and they are often painted on ceilings or in small passages where they would be difficult if not almost impossible to see. If we look at a plan of the cave of Lascaux (Plate I-41), we see that there are paintings in an extremely narrow passageway, while at Altamira many are in a small area that could hold few people at a time (Plate I-42). All this suggests to the trained anthropologist one theory above all others: that the purpose of the paintings and reliefs was magic. It is thought that the pictures were made as part of the magic rites necessary to ensure the supply of game for food and clothing, and to secure success in the chase. Among all primitive peoples, even today, the likeness or image of anything living, human or animal, is thought to be just as real as its model. African Bushmen and Pygmies make drawings of the animals they are going to hunt and shoot arrows at the pictures to make sure of a kill. So the purpose of prehistoric men in making pictures of animals was to win magical control over them, turning the quarry into the victim and giving greater confidence to the hunters. The animals in the cave paintings are usually those which were killed as game, not the more formidable beasts of prey. On the whole, individual animals are shown, though male and female animals are sometimes painted following each other. Possibly the reason why fish are seldom painted is that they could be harpooned easily without the invocation of magic; bones of seafish are quite common among Magdalenian remains. For all his skill in tracking and spear-throwing, ancient man, equipped only with arrows and flint-and-bone-headed lances, must have found hunting a constant source of anxiety.

The artist, who was also a magician, performed a function of vital importance to his people. As surely as the picture of an

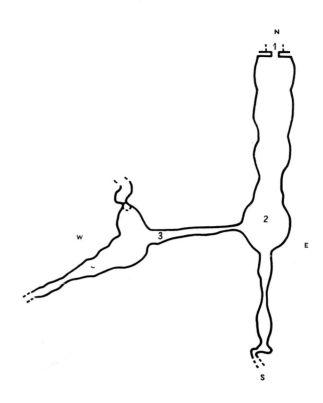

I-41. **Plan of the Lascaux caves, Dordogne, France. Showing: 1. Entrance; 2. Hall of the Bulls; 3. Passage with painted walls.**

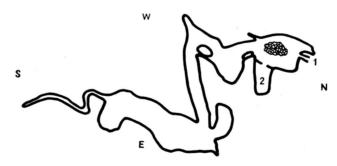

I-42. **Plan of the cave of Altamira, Santander, Spain. Showing: 1. Entrance; 2. Cave of Prehistoric paintings.**

animal appeared on the cave wall, conjured up by sure and skillful strokes of the primitive paint brush or engraving tool, so surely would the real animal appear, to be killed by the hunters and archers of the tribe. The hunting motive in prehistoric art is made clear by representations of arrows and spears piercing the bodies of the animals, like those sticking in the flanks of a bison and ibex in the Black Hall cave at Niaux, and wounding horses and bison at Lascaux. Some of the most vivid and moving paintings are of wounded and dying animals. At Montespan, clay models of a lion and bear have been found with the marks of stabbing by spears, together with a bear's skull, which must mean that a ritual killing in mime had taken place. On the walls of certain caves are painted dancing figures of men masked as animals; they are wearing a bison's horns, or the mask and antlers of a red deer, or the tail of a wolf or horse similar to the ceremonial dress of African medicine men. It seems most likely that dances and miming by masked figures, probably the magicians themselves, were part of the magic rituals performed in the innermost depths of limestone caverns sometimes a mile or more beneath the earth. This *sympathetic* magic of which we speak may have had other purposes than the mere killing of prey. The pregnant female fertility figures are also examples of the artist's portrayal of a desired event. Animals, too, may have been portrayed in a pregnant state in the hope that they would multiply, and pictures may have been painted to propitiate the spirit of a dead and vengeful animal.

Daylight never penetrates the darkness of these caves, which in some cases are accessible today only by climbing, crawling, and underwater swimming. The achievement of the artist-magicians seems all the more extraordinary considering they had to work by the flickering light of torches made of some resinous branch, or by the feeble flames of animal fat burning in rough stone lamps with moss wicks. Some of these stone lamps have been found in the caves. But then, as we have seen, the artists were trained craftsmen of great experience. Man, at this point in history, may have felt that his very survival depended on the artist's skill.

Most extraordinary of all, an aura of magic lingers around many of these caves to this very day. Often, the natives of the areas fear the caves. Christian monks in the Baltic, for example, painted crosses over certain rock paintings to destroy their power, in which the local population must have strongly believed. Other cave areas, such as Lourdes in France, were turned into Christian places of worship. All this suggests a *folk* memory, kept alive by word-of-mouth tales stretching perhaps thirty millennia into the "great backward and abyss of time."

By 10,000 B.C. the ice sheets which had covered northern Europe were slowly receding, and by 8000 B.C. they had finally contracted. Tundra and steppe gave way to stunted vegetation, then to pine and fir trees, followed by birch, ash, and oak. As the forests encroached, the herds of reindeer, bison, and mammoth disappeared, and with them the brilliant culture of the Magdalenian hunters.

With the breaking-up of the Paleolithic world a new pattern of hunter-fisher life emerged in the forest clearings and seashores, now free from ice. Deer and smaller game took the place of the huge Paleolithic beasts, axes for felling trees were invented, fishing tackle became more elaborate, and the bow appeared. And so there followed what is called the Mesolithic period, or

Middle Stone Age (from 10,000 to 3500 B.C. in Europe), and eventually the Neolithic period, or New Stone Age (from 3500 to 1700 B.C. in Europe).

But the true, imaginative art of the hunter of the mammoth died with the beasts themselves. Mesolithic art of caves like that at Cogul on the eastern Spanish coast is quite different. Here the artists painted full scenes comprised of hunters, warriors, and dancers, but the figures are brittle, flat, and stick-like forms and seem stylized, as if one were copied from another according to a conventional pattern, rather than from the observation of nature.

The last of the great rock paintings are to be found, not in Europe at all, but in what is now the dry and lifeless expanse of the Sahara. It was not always so. Before 4000 B.C. this area was lush and well-watered. Then the rain belt shifted northward, and as the temperate zone became warmer, North Africa became hotter and more desiccated, and animal and human populations were driven toward the valleys and moist uplands.

The rock art of the Sahara shows us that in Neolithic times many cultures flourished there. Along the southern side of the Atlas Mountains are cave paintings of elephants, giraffes, lions, and a type of giant buffalo now extinct. The largest number of paintings can be found in the region of Tassili n'Ajjer, northeast of the Hoggar and reaching the Fezzan on the east. It is a sandstone plateau, difficult to reach, with narrow passages cutting through rock cliffs. These once provided natural homes for the early inhabitants who left hundreds of paintings on the walls of their former dwellings.

The more ancient of these paintings are the work of Negro artists. These are often carefully organized compositions of many figures, human and animal alike, in scenes

I-43. **Rock painting of men and cattle, from Tassili in the Sahara.**

of hunting, fighting, and daily life. The picture in Plate I-43 can be dated from about 4000 B.C., when the Saharan peoples abandoned hunting to become cattle breeders and herdsmen. The silhouetted figures of men are natural and graceful, and the cattle are painted with the utmost delicacy. The viewer can see at a glance that they are domesticated and not the wild animals of the caves of Lascaux and Altamira. Plate I-44 shows what may be a hunting scene, with female figures performing a ritual dance in the background, and smaller figures who seem to be fighting. The whole picture, with its lively composition and grouping, has a narrative character, as if illustrating an actual event, and this is typical of North African rock painting. Like the later painters of the eastern Spanish coast, but unlike the painters of the great Paleolithic works, the Saharan artists understood the notion of a composition comprising many figures. They were masters, too, of action. The little figures in Plate I-45 are intent on some ritual, or they are possibly hunting or tracking an animal, and each

I-44. **Rock painting, from Tassili in the Sahara.**

I-45. **Rock painting of a ritual, a hunt, or a tracking expedition, from Tassili in the Sahara.**

gesture is realistic and meaningful. The figures in Plate I-46 are evidently chasing an animal quarry or an enemy. There is a great impression of speed and urgency as, bow in hand, they literally fly through the air.

The later Saharan paintings show some Egyptian influence, and so these works bring us to the dawn of what we think of as civilization, and yet if we look back over the millennia to the works of the cave painters of the Paleolithic period, we can only regard them with amazement. Early man must have hunted tirelessly to find his pigments, and spent laborious hours fashion-

I-46. **Rock painting of figures chasing animal quarry or an enemy, from Tassili in the Sahara.**

ing his brushes and implements. He styled, using a technique that took perhaps thousands of years to develop, paintings and sculpture that were not merely realistic, but which gave aesthetic pleasure to the viewer; and he did this at a time when his social organization was the most simple and his daily nourishment depended on what nuts and berries he could find in the forest or what game he tracked down and killed with the most basic of weapons. What kind of men were these? In our imagination we see them as existing in an almost animal state, and yet in spirit some of them were artists of great taste. Look at the charmingly sketched wild cow from Altamira (Plate I-27). The artist has not been literal. With a delicate, yet sure line he has sketched the alert tilt of the cow's ears, her bovine eye and wrinkled muzzle, her heavy neck and slender legs. When we look at this work we can only ask—could the artist have seen the world so very differently from the way we see it? Could he have been so very different from ourselves?

FOR PERHAPS a million years men had been living as hunters, wholly dependent on what nature provided for shelter, clothing, and food, keeping always on the move in the search for fresh hunting lands. And then, after the last great Ice Age, man began to change his habits. From about 7000 B.C., he turned slowly from a hunting and food gathering way of life to a farming life in settled villages.

This change, called the *Neolithic Revolution,* brought in the New Stone Age. Man now began to use polished flints and axes in place of the unpolished stone and flint implements of Paleolithic times. But far more important, at this time it was discovered that the seeds of certain wild plants would take root and grow if deliberately planted. Along with the cultivation of crops, man also learned the taming and breeding of useful animals, and developed the art of pottery and the weaving of cloth.

The Neolithic Revolution took place over a great range of time, and it happened more swiftly in some places than in others. Beginning from eight to nine thousand years ago in its cradleland, southwest Asia, it took between three and four thousand years to reach as far as Europe in one direction and China in the other. Well before the end of this period men had advanced to what we call full civilization, with well-organized village, town, and even national life, in Palestine, Syria, Anatolia, Iraq, Iran, and the valleys of the Indus and the Nile, although in Europe they were still living in primitive conditions.

It was between 4000 and 3000 B.C. that many exciting changes took place in certain parts of the world. Men discovered the art of making bricks and building with them, and they developed uses for the wheel. They learned, too, to harness animals to carry or haul heavy weights, and to make a ship move through the water with the aid of a sail. With these discoveries men began to specialize. It took skill to create fine pottery or to build a sailing ship, and a man would have to abandon farming to learn such a skill. The artists of the Old Stone Age had perhaps been the first craftsmen, but now there were many more. It was at this time, too, that a most important discovery was made: that copper could be separated from ores and forged into a cutting surface sharper than flint, and that it could be combined with tin to form bronze. With these discoveries man moved into the Bronze Age.

These new developments took root quickly in the valley of the Nile. Here the conditions for thriving life were as good as anywhere on earth. The sun beat down from a cloudless sky on a river that rose like clockwork every year, depositing rich soil in its valley and ensuring a good crop. Moreover, this enchanted valley, a warm place where little clothing and shelter were needed, was miraculously protected from invaders that might descend on its wealth. On all sides save the north where it was bounded by the sea, there stretched vast, seemingly endless deserts. These deserts were as rich in their way as the valley itself. In them, the Egyptians were able to find the ores of not only copper but gold, and the hard stone from which they eventually honed their everlasting statues and monu-

II-1. **Terra-cotta pottery of the black-top type.   Predynastic period.**

ments: diorite, quartzite, and granite, as well as many gems.   These deserts could be crossed with great care by caravans of traders who stopped at the widely separated and easily controlled oases, but they were a terrifying barrier to an invading army.

Although conditions were good, they were not quite perfect.   There was little rainfall in the valley of the Nile, and at some point the inhabitants must have started making dikes and cutting canals to control the flood waters and irrigate their land.   They could only manage this kind of work if several villages cooperated.   In time one of

these gained power over its neighbors.   So it was, in all probability, the need for channeling water to the land that caused the Egyptians to be among the first to unite small communities into larger political units.

From the very first the Egyptians were talented craftsmen and artists.   Moreover, because of the dry climate and sandy soil of much of Egypt, remnants of Egyptian culture are left from the very earliest times. The fine terra-cotta (fired clay) pottery of the black-top type we see in Plate II-1 is thin and elegant in shape.   It is called *black-top* work because these vases have a broad black stripe around the mouth in contrast with the light red of the rest of the vase. The method of making such vases was rather complicated. The potter coated each one with hematite, a reddish-colored ferrous compound, and blackened the mouth by surrounding it with straw which was carbonized slowly. The terra-cotta vases with wavy handles of a somewhat later period (Plate II-2) are similar to those found in Palestine, while the vases in Plate II-3, tinted a light brown, are decorated with stylized paintings of boats, plants, and animals in a reddish color. They represent perhaps the earliest attempt at landscape painting ever made. The ivory and bone pins and comb, rings and bracelets in Plates II-4 and II-5 show the excellence of Egyptian craftsmanship before the use of metals.

Ivory was obtained from the hippopotamuses which infested the Nile, and we see an alabaster figurine of one of these lumbering animals in Plate II-6. The cave artists were also sculptors of great talent, but here, I think, we see a bit of humor. The slate palette (Plate II-7), used for mixing the green paint which women used as a cosmetic around their eyes, with its fish shape and one fishy eye, shows a similar economy and wit. But it was in portraying the human body that the early Egyptians excelled all those who had gone before, not merely as craftsmen but as artists. The ivory figurine in Plate II-8 is a far cry from the bulbous fertility goddesses of the Stone Age. This slender and beautifully formed figure shows that the sculptor has captured the basic grace of the human body. The figurine in

II-2. **Two terra-cotta jars with wavy handles. Predynastic period.**

II-3. **Terra-cotta vases decorated with stylized paintings. Predynastic period.**

II-4. Ivory and bone pins and comb. Predynastic period.

II-5. Ivory and bone rings and bracelets. Predynastic period.

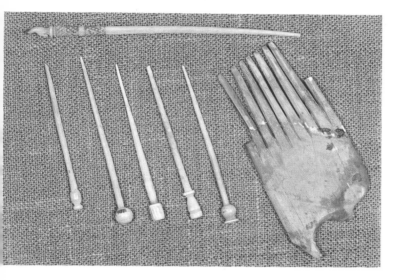

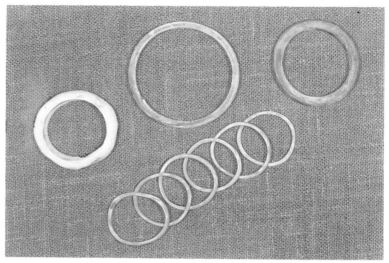

II-6. Alabaster hippopotamus. *c.* 3000 B.C.

II-7. Slate palette in the form of a fish. Predynastic period.

Plate II-9 amuses us at first. While this figure, with her shoulders hunched, arms cramped and confined to the body, and face indicated by a few incised lines, is not as well made or finished as the other, we see here for the first time hair worn down to the shoulders in the traditional Egyptian style we shall see for centuries to come. At first the little figurine looks as if she is squinting at us through huge blue sunglasses. This inlay of lapis lazuli, a blue semiprecious stone highly prized by the Egyptians, represents the lady's eyes, lavishly smeared as they must have been with blue eyeshadow.

The fragment of painted fabric in Plate II-10 should interest us. The linen, made of very fine thread, took four years to reassemble, and it tells us many things. For one thing, it tells us that, even before their history actually began, the Egyptians were making fine textiles, of linen in any case. Cotton and silk were not known until much later times, and wool was considered unsuitable for clothing. Depicted on this fragment of cloth we see two boats on the Nile. These boats, although manned by little stick figures, seem extraordinarily developed. They must have been very large, as long rows of oarsmen can be seen on each side, and they have a steersman and cabin space on deck. Such boats were absolutely necessary from the earliest time, because in ancient Egypt there was only one way to travel—by boat—and only one highway—the Nile.

If we look at a map of Egypt (Plate II-11) we see that the Nile runs through the land for 600 miles, and yet the cultivated area was no more than about 10 miles wide, except at the Delta where the river fans out into a great triangle of many waterways, inlets, and tributaries. Here much of the land is swampy and filled with great thickets

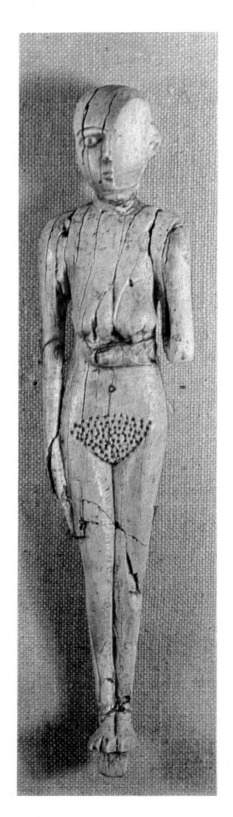

II-8. Ivory figurine of a woman. Predynastic period.

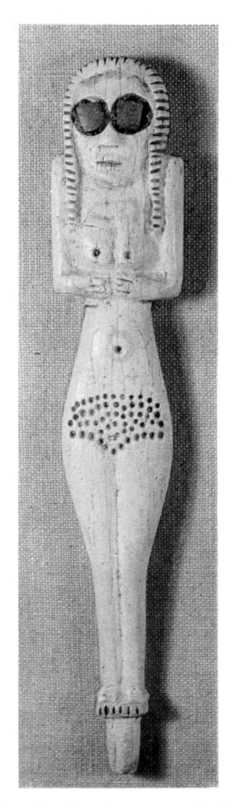

II-9. Ivory figurine of a woman. Predynastic period.

of papyrus. The earliest and simplest Egyptian boats were skiffs made of these papyrus plants (which stood as tall as a man) tied together. It was in this northern Delta land that what herds there were in Egypt grazed, and vines were tended to produce an excellent wine, although beer made from grain was the staple drink. The Delta also possessed seaports from which the Egyptians could trade with the eastern Mediterranean—Crete, the Aegean, and Palestine. Needless to say, conditions in the Delta were different from those in the riverbank region to the south. At the dawn of history these two regions formed two separate kingdoms, the Kingdom of Lower Egypt (the Delta), and Upper Egypt (the Nile valley). It was with the unification of these two under King Nar-mer (or Menes) of Upper Egypt, around 3200 B.C., that recorded history began.

By the time King Nar-mer ruled the entire of united Egypt, its culture had reached extraordinary heights. Not only were there many superbly made objects found in the tombs of the period—fine carpentry, beautiful jewelry, and sculpted and painted works of all kinds—but the Egyptians had begun to master the art of writing and the sciences of recording and measurement, architecture, mathematics, astronomy, and planned agriculture. They were a literate, thinking people.

How had this highly developed culture come about? The objects which have been found, such as those we have seen, tell us only bits of the story. They do not tell us how writing was developed, or how the ship depicted on linen was first built, or how the linen was first made. All this appears to come out of nowhere. What, then, is the answer to the mystery of Egyptian civilization? I will tell you two quite

II-10. Fragment of painted fabric from a tomb at El Gebelein.   Predynastic period.

different theories, of the many that scholars hold.

One is that Egyptian culture developed not in Upper Egypt, where evidence remained preserved for millennia in the dry sands, but rather in the steamy Delta. It was much easier, we must remember, for the peoples of the Delta, with their seaports, to exchange ideas with the outside world, such as it then was.   We know that before the age of Nar-mer and the First Dynasty, the Delta possessed a Great Port into which came timber from the Lebanon, tall timber for building masts such as could not be found in Egypt. But all traces of the development of shipbuilding left in the Delta would have been lost. Objects that have lasted five thousand years in the deserts to the south would decay quickly if buried in the swampy deposits of the Delta. In fact, almost all that we do know of ancient Egypt at its height we learned from what was to be found in the dry desert cliffs bordering the great valley of Upper Egypt, the cliffs on the edge of the cultivated land, which the Egyptians mined for limestone and near which they built their temples and tombs. In the Delta the fields are flat and unmarked.

The second possibility is that Egypt was invaded from without by a people, possibly from Mesopotamia, the Land of the Two Rivers to the east, who brought much of this learning with them. This theory is supported by certain works of art. One of the best examples is a knife handle from Gebel el Arak (Plate II-12), dating from about the time of the unification. The blade shows the perfection of prehistoric flint work, but the ivory handle is one of the first examples of relief carving found in Egypt. On one side we see a hero standing between two lions, and on the other we see what appears to be a battle at sea between typical Egyptian ships and those of strangers. These have a high prow and look suspiciously like the ships of the river Tigris in Mesopotamia. What tale does this tell? There are other works too: slate palettes, at first made for mixing cosmetics and eventually used as tablets to commemorate political and military events. Some that have been found seem to represent stages in a war between Upper and Lower Egypt. In Plates II-13 and II-14 the lion and bull respectively, attacking and trampling vanquished enemies, symbolize the powers of

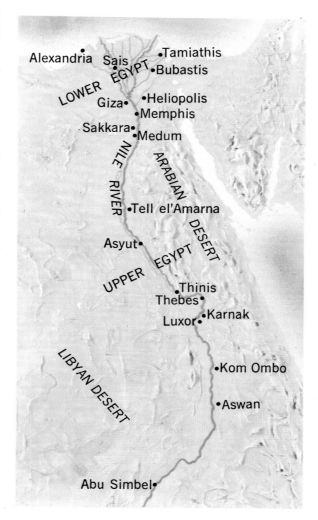

II-11. **Map of Egypt.**

the rulers of the south. We have not yet studied the varying styles of relief in Egypt and her powerful neighbors in Mesopotamia, but it suffices to say that the figures on the knife handle and palettes have the bulky, chunky, rounded relief, the woolly hair and bearded faces we will see in the works of Mesopotamia. Does this indicate some Mesopotamian invasion early in the history of Egypt? The burial sites of a people of a different physical type from the native Egyptians, dating from about this time, shortly before the First Dynasty, have also been found. But while this art resembles that of Mesopotamia, it is also very different. The truth is that we do not know where these people came from, whether they invaded or slowly infiltrated the local population, whether they brought the arts of writing, mathematics, and architecture with them, or whether in fact these came from outside at all. And so the historical period in Egypt opens with a mystery, the first of many.

What we do know is that Egyptian history dawned with a splendid culture, and one of the first great monuments of that culture is the great palette or tablet of Nar-mer (Plate II-15), commemorating the unification itself. Here we see Nar-mer wearing the tall and tubular white crown of Upper Egypt and brandishing a mace over his defeated enemy. His name is written above in hieroglyphs between two heads of Hat-hor, the cow-goddess. A Horus falcon is perched on a clump of papyrus holding in its human hand a cord which tethers a bearded head, forming the end of the land out of which the plants grow. This means, "The king, the incarna-

**II-12. Knife from Gebel el Arak.** *c.* 3000 B.C.

II-14. Slate palette carved in relief showing a bull attacking a fallen enemy. Predynastic period.

II-13. Palette carved in relief showing a lion attacking a fallen enemy. Predynastic period.

45

tion of the Hawk-god, Horus, with his strong right arm leads captive the marsh-dwellers"; in other words, the north has been conquered by the state god of the south, whose embodiment on earth is Nar-mer.

On the other side Nar-mer can be seen wearing the red crown of Lower Egypt and marching with his standard bearers to view the bound and decapitated bodies of his northern enemies. The story could not be more clear. And from this time forward the kings of Egypt will call themselves King of Upper and Lower Egypt and will wear the double crown, a combination of the crowns of Upper and Lower Egypt, symbolized by the serpent and the vulture.

The unification of Egypt marked the beginning of the First Dynasty, a dynasty being a period during which Egypt was ruled by a single family. A change of the family holding the throne meant a change of dynasty, and there were some thirty dynasties in the three thousand years during which ancient Egypt flourished. The first twenty dynasties were divided yet again into long general periods which we refer to as the Old, Middle, and New Kingdoms (Plate II-16). These, we shall see, were separated more by political events than by cultural developments. Much that was greatest in Egyptian culture and art was already present in the glorious days of the Old Kingdom.

What kind of people were the ancient Egyptians? Having read of pharaohs who ruled with the power of a god, mummies, curses, and books of the dead, the reader may well approach the subject with a mixture of fascination and fear. He may be surprised to find he is dealing with a people who loved swimming pools and vintage wine. The life of the ancient Egyptians

II-15. **The tablet of Nar-mer.** **First Dynasty.**

was, in fact, as peaceful as that of any people in history, and full of sunshine.

The average Egyptian was a peasant who tilled the soil, but this is not to say that his was a life of poverty and misery. Actual peasants' homes, which were made of mud-brick and easily obliterated by time, have not been found, but we have the remains of an entire town of workmen's houses, and these could not have been very different. They are much more comfortable than we might expect, with four rooms—an entrance area, a large family room, a kitchen, and a storeroom or extra bedroom. On hot nights the family might sleep on the flat roof. The house was sensibly built for a warm climate with thick walls and few windows. If it was a farmer's house, there would probably be a garden behind. In the evening the family would enjoy a hearty meal of bread, beer, beans, and lentils, the root vegetables, onions and leeks, and possibly fish, followed by figs, dates, and grapes. Meat was admittedly scarce, although not unknown.

But not all Egyptians were peasants. If one trained, one might learn a craft or even become an artist of rank. There were many craftsmen: bakers and fishermen, carpenters and weavers, sculptors and stone masons. But if a boy strove for higher things, the craft to learn was that of scribe.

The scribe was trained in the art of reading and writing (as well as simple mathematics), and this was the key to all advancement. Scribes were not merely secretaries who could take dictation; eventually all positions in the administration of the country, from tax collector to grand vizier or high priest, were open to the intelligent scribe. Small wonder boys at school were made to write laboriously, over and over again, "More beneficial is writing than the house of a builder, or tombs in the west.

| EGYPT | | |
|---|---|---|
| **Neolithic Age** | c. 7000-3200 B.C. | predynastic |
| **Thinite Dynasties** Capital: Thinis | c. 3200-2685 B.C. | I-II dynasties |
| **Old Kingdom** Capital: Memphis | 2685-2280 B.C. | III-VI dynasties |
| 1st Intermediary Period | 2280-2060 B.C. | VII-X dynasties |
| **Middle Kingdom** Capital: Thebes | 2060-1650 B.C. | XI-XIII dynasties |
| 2nd Intermediary Period | 1650-1580 B.C. | XV-XVII dynasties |
| **New Kingdom** Capital: Thebes | 1580-1085 B.C. | XVIII-XX dynasties |
| **Anarchy** foreign domination | 1085-332 B.C. | XXI-XXX dynasties |
| **Greek Period** Capital: Alexandria | 332-30 A.D. | |

II-16. **Historical periods of Ancient Egypt.**

It is better than an established fortress, or a tombstone in the temple."[1]

But reading and writing Egyptian script was not that easy a matter. Egyptian writing started as a series of pictographs, symbolic pictures representing such simple objects as a man or a hand. Then such symbols, or hieroglyphs, were used to represent the sounds of these words when they formed parts of other words, and a type of alpha-

[1] Barbara Mertz, *Red Land, Black Land,* Coward McCann Inc., New York, 1966, p. 136

47

betic script developed. By the beginning of the First Dynasty a freer, cursive form of hieroglyphic writing was also in use. But with the vast number of symbols and the complication of a writing in which there are no symbols for vowel sounds, the task of the Egyptian schoolboy could not have been easy. It must have been in taking endless dictation that he learned some literature, history, and religious teachings.

There were other matters for the young scribe to learn as well, necessary for becoming a member of the huge bureaucracy that administered Egypt. Only well-trained civil servants could organize large-scale irrigation, land reclamation, and tax collection. Receipts and expenditures, the work of the state, all needed to be recorded, and for this the scribe had to know mathematics and measurement. Standard measures for assessing the amount of the wheat harvest were devised, and a method of accurate survey was worked out for reestablishing boundaries between fields after they had been erased by the flood. But learning such complicated matters was well worthwhile. Although the sons of craftsmen tended to follow in their fathers' steps, and the sons of scribes as well, there was no rule of inherited profession. By the Fifth Dynasty, probably any boy with intelligence and energy could become an official. And the life of a high official at court, like that of a landowner, was pleasant indeed. He might have a house with many airy apartments (complete with clean bathrooms and other facilities), decorated with wall paintings and reliefs and surrounded by courts and gardens with beds of flowers and pools of fresh water. Servants waited on his every need, and his dinner menu was delicious. He might have duck or goose, which were hunted in the papyrus swamps and not do-

mesticated; beef or lamb; sweets made of honey; fruits like the apricot; and the finest of wines, carefully marked with the year of its vintage. And, as we shall see, he would be assured all of these good things in the life to come.

On top of the great Egyptian social pyramid sat the king, at once chief administrator and god. How did the king succeed to the throne? Oddly enough, despite the fact that we know so much about ancient Egypt and especially about the kings, whose lives and acts were depicted so often by ancient artists, we do not know the answer to this simple question. It may be that descent to the throne went through the female line, or that it went to the king's sons by his official wife, the queen, and if the queen had only daughters, to a daughter's husband. In this case the husband would be chosen from among the king's children by his concubines, so the succession would not leave the family. Again, there is a perplexing mystery.

Technically, all Egypt belonged to the king, or pharaoh, and in fact his personal wealth was past all reckoning. The palace and its official buildings was the Great House, or *Per-o,* from which the Hebrew word *pharaoh* was derived. Government was carried on here by the king's highest chosen officials. His life, like that of his courtiers, seems to have been one of pleasures in moderation, and although his power was absolute, he does not seem to have had much taste for the cruel excesses practiced by later Oriental and Roman monarchs. To the people, he was god incarnated as king, who sustained and protected them, and he had command over the Nile in a rainless land. Nar-mer or Menes, for example, the traditional founder of the First Dynasty, is described on his palette as the incarnation of the Hawk-god, Horus. He is credited with damming the Nile and founding Memphis, the new capital of the united Egypt, at the point where the river branches into the Delta. Such monumental undertakings were considered suitable work for the pharaohs, about whom we know a great deal, and yet in some ways very little.

To understand Egyptian art, we must first understand Egyptian religion, and this was quite unlike any that came before or since. We may suppose that each village along the river had, in prehistoric times, one or several gods, and as the land was gradually unified no god was discarded, so that by historical times, the Egyptians worshiped innumerable deities. Some they visualized in human form, some in animal form, some in combined human and animal form, and some in two or three forms all at once. Not only did the powers of these gods overlap, but they often borrowed each other's powers and emblems. Moreover, the Egyptians were nothing if not broad-minded, and were always pleased to adopt foreign gods and add them to their already over-populated pantheon. A list of just a few of the most important deities will give you some idea of the colorful confusion: Amun was god of the air, always shown in human form, although the ram and goose were sacred to him; Re was a sun-god, also shown in human form, to whom the falcon was sacred; Osiris was god of the dead, shown in the form of a human mummy; Isis was Osiris' wife, depicted sometimes as a woman and sometimes as her sacred animal, the cow; Horus was a hawk-headed god often seen as guardian of the king (the son of Isis and Osiris was also called Horus); Ptah was the god of artisans, always seen in human form; Hat-hor was the goddess of love, and like Isis her sacred animal was the cow; and so on.

The religion itself comprised everything we consider correctly or mistakenly associated with religion today, a great mass of superstitions, magic spells, and actual philosophic doctrine. The myths the Egyptians wove about their gods remind us in many ways of the myths of ancient Greece. They are charming and often confusing, although rarely frightening. But Greek mythology was worked into a single system. There was one story of creation, one account of the rising and setting of the sun, each god had his specific powers, and for every phenomenon known to man there was one explanation. The Egyptians, on the other hand, might have half a dozen totally different tales to explain the most simple occurrence. These were later supplemented by complex philosophical theories.

One of the most important of all Egyptian myths was the story of Osiris: Osiris came to the throne of his father, Geb, god of the earth, and ruled the world justly with his wife Isis, who was also his sister. But his brother Seth was jealous, so he slew Osiris and cut up his body in many pieces, which he buried all over Egypt. But his loving wife set out with her sister Nephthys to search for the pieces, and with the aid of Anubis, the jackal god of cemeteries, the pieces were put together and Osiris brought back to life. He then went to rule in the Underworld, where he passed final judgment on dead souls. Meanwhile, Isis bore a son, Horus, who defeated Seth and won back his throne.

This seems a familiar enough tale. We have seen the elements in a dozen myths from different nations: the ruler who is slain by his brother for his throne, and whose son takes vengeance for his father and wins it back. But this is also a story of death and resurrection, and this was of great importance to the Egyptians, because more

II-17. **Ivory lion. First Dynasty.**

than any other people they were obsessed with the idea of life after death, and this was the wellspring of their greatest art.

The ancient Egyptians' preoccupation with death is what accounts for any notion we may have that their civilization was gloomy, but this was not at all so. In fact, they were more optimistic about death than any people in history. They simply didn't believe in it. They were convinced that if the body of the dead man were carefully preserved and provided for, his soul, which had several forms, would continue to live in the Land of Eternity, the Beautiful Roads of the West, the Field of Offerings, the Marsh of Reeds, the Court of Re across the Lily Lake . . . their notions of the next world were often as beautiful and as vague as our own. But they were sure that the soul could live there forever, if it were provided in the next world with everything it needed on earth. At first this rebirth was reserved for the king and those who served him, but later in Egyptian history it was possible for anyone.

It was not a new idea. From the time of the Stone Age, men were buried with weapons and trinkets, clearly on the theory that they were going somewhere where they would need them. But the Egyptians carried this notion to unheard of lengths. The body of the departed was carefully mummified, a technique which took centuries to develop. According to the perfected method, the body was treated for seventy days with a dehydrating salt, and then wrapped in many layers of linen bandages. It was then placed in a tomb with food, clothing, cosmetics, furniture, games (the small ivory lion in Plate II-17 may actually have been a piece in a board game), and every household object it might need. If it were a child's body, it was given toys. But most important to us, the walls of the tombs were covered with reliefs and paintings of everything the dead man had enjoyed in life. Did he love to hunt in the papyrus swamp? Did he love to play with his children or sit at dinner with his wife and listen to music? These things were carefully portrayed. He would need servants to cultivate his lands and bake his bread. These, too, were depicted on the walls, and little figurines, or *shawabty*-figures representing the servants, along with tiny model houses and boats were also placed in the grave. The ivory statuette of a female slave (Plate II-18) is such a figure. Both it and the little ivory lion date from the First Dynasty, and they are more natural and realistic than much of the later work we shall see. On the walls, too, were written spells and advice to the soul which would help him find his way to the next world and help him pass the final judgment. Much later these spells were compiled into what is known as the *Book of the Dead,* and they assist the soul in every possible way. They even tell him how to get his *shawabty*-figures to work. One false step, and he might die a second time, a fate from which there was no salvation.

But how, to the Egyptians, could pictures serve the purpose of tangible objects and live people? By the very "sympathetic magic" by which the cave man expected a live buffalo to come to take the place of his painted one. So anxious were they to supply the dead man with a future in a world as charming and as full of life as the one he was leaving that they achieved what is the object of much great art, the successful, pleasing, and vivid portrayal of the attractions of this world.

We can see this world, superbly depicted, in the very earliest reliefs from the walls of tombs of the Old Kingdom. Of the first two dynasties, the Archaic period in Egypt, we know very little, historically. But with the founding of the Third Dynasty (about 2685 B.C.) by King Djoser, the Old Kingdom begins, and by this time the style of Egyptian art had already been per-

II-18. **Ivory statuette of a female slave. First Dynasty.**

II-19. **Wooden panel from the tomb of Hesy-re, described as a "scribe and acquaintance of the king," near Sakkareh. Third Dynasty.**

fected to a degree it rarely surpassed. In fact, the earliest art of the Old Kingdom remained typical of Egyptian art throughout its history, for as we shall see, artistic styles changed little for three thousand years.

Hesy-re is described as a "scribe and acquaintance of the king." In the wooden panel relief in Plate II-19 we see him sitting proudly, his rod of office in one hand and his writing materials on his back: a small pot for water, the long palette for holding pens, and two rounded cakes of solid ink—black, made of carbon, and red, made of ocher. He is surrounded by pictographs representing his various possessions, including everyday utensils.

But although the figure and the pictographs surrounding it are carved with superb elegance and finish, we notice something strange about the way the figure is represented. The fact is that for all the superb finish of Egyptian art, the Egyptians never cared to deal with the problems of perspective and foreshortening, that is, the representation of an object receding in space. So rather than struggle with the problem of depicting a nose as seen from the front, they would paint or carve a face in profile, with the eye as seen frontally. Shoulders, on the other hand, were represented as seen from the front, as the side view of a shoulder presents the most complicated foreshortening problem of all. Knees and feet seen from the front would present the same problem, and so they are seen in profile, with a gentle and gradual twist at the waist. On two other panels (Plates II-20 and II-21) we see the resolute figure of Hesy-re, his beaky nose and thick lips quite recognizable, similarly portrayed, although he is standing. Only his elaborate hair style is changed, as he wears a variety of wigs, usually made of human hair.

This method of representing the human figure, once set, remained the fashion until ancient Egyptian culture came to an end, and so we say that Egyptian art was *stylized*. By this we mean it followed a set pattern in the representation of certain (although not all) things, and that the artist did not experiment constantly to approach visual reality. The way we see Hesy-re represented, with head in profile and shoulders in frontal position, was not only accepted, it was the way the Egyptians expected to see the human body portrayed for three millennia. In fact, whatever the origin of these rules, they remained in effect because they satisfied another requirement of great importance to the Egyptian—that as much of the figure be seen as possible: both arms, both legs, front and back. For magical purposes, it was important to represent a complete image of the human being, instead of merely recording a momentary visual image. Thus the action of the figure can be clearly "read." Usually, the distortion is not even disconcerting, so skillful were the artists in uniting the parts in a decorative whole. The rules were the same for all representation of three dimensions in two dimensions, whether it be painting or low relief.

The panels from the tomb of Hesy-re were originally set in the doors of niches in the brick superstructure of the burial pit. They are not representative Egyptian reliefs in that they are carved in wood, rather than in the limestone of which the decorated walls of Egyptian tombs, temples, and palaces were made. The painted limestone stele, or tombstone, in Plate II-22, or the stone relief of Geb, the Earth-god, in Plate II-23, although artistically less interesting, are more typical work. The relief sculptor's task was a complicated one: the figure was carefully blocked out on a grid-iron plan marked on the stone surface, so that all figures had the same proportions (the head so many squares in size, the arm so many squares long, etc.). This was done by an outline draftsman. Then the relief sculptor cut away the background. Sometimes, as in the case of the relief from the tomb of Ti in Plate II-24, the figures were sunken beneath the level of the surface, which was not cut away. Then the figures and all details were skillfully painted. Here, too, styles or conventions were to be followed. A man's skin was generally painted a reddish color, a woman's more yellow. Hair was black and clothing white, with color generally added by brilliant jewelry.

Most of the painting has come off the relief from the tomb of Ti, as it has from the wooden panels of Hesy-re, but in other places we shall see it better preserved.

Painting was done with reed stems splayed out at the ends and palm-fiber brushes. As in the cave paintings, black was achieved with carbon, and red and yellow with ocher. But the Egyptians had a much greater variety of colors, such as green and blue, which were made from various minerals like malachite or azurite and powdered enamel. These pigments were mixed with some adhesive. We are not sure what it generally was, but in some cases it was probably beeswax, although this may have been used as a coating.

II-20. **Wooden panel from the tomb of Hesy-re, near Sakkareh. Third Dynasty.**

II-21. **Wooden panel from the tomb of Hesy-re, near Sakkareh. Third Dynasty.**

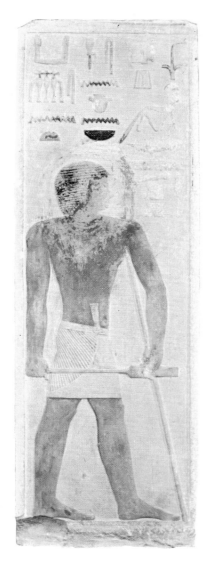

II-23. Limestone relief of Geb, the Earth-god, from the shrine of King Djoser at Heliopolis. Third Dynasty.

II-22. Painted limestone stele. *c.* 2600 B.C.

Ti and Hesy-re were noblemen, and they were represented in much the same way, and in the same dignified poses, although they lived two centuries apart. People of rank, in fact, are rarely seen in any pose other than sitting or standing majestically awaiting eternity, unless they are seen kneeling before a pharaoh. It is in the pictures of servants, whose sole purpose was to work for all eternity, that the artist was able to give his figures energy and life. And here we see that he could, within the bounds of the Egyptian stylization, make his figures do virtually anything.

On another wall of the tomb of Ti, we see a servant goading asses to trample grain on the threshing floor (Plate II-25). The asses have a certain naturalistic charm, for it was in portraying animals and children that Egyptian art could be the most lively and touching.

A great many tombs of noblemen of the

II-24. Relief from the tomb of Ti at Sakkareh. *c.* 2500 B.C.

Old Kingdom have been found, generally belonging to some provincial governor or high official, like Ti or Hesy-re. In them we find reliefs which give the impression of the teeming life of Egyptian country people. They are shown sowing and reaping crops, tending their animals, grinding corn, fishing in the Nile, hunting in the papyrus swamp, and preparing food for the lord of the estate for whom they worked. In the relief in Plate II-26 from the tomb of Akhty-hotpe, the servants are quartering an ox. The great arching line of the ox's head and horn make it a thing of beauty, even in its unhappy plight, and the servants move with the rhythmic grace of dancers. In Plate II-27, we see Akhty-hotpe's servants carrying ducks and geese, on which he will feast eternally. In the relief from the tomb of the vizier Merer-wy-kuy (Plate II-28), we see the man himself standing upright in the prow of a small skiff and catching by the tail an animal which is trying to reach a bird's nest. And here we see a typical Egyptian scheme for presenting the whole visual world: the earth, what is beneath, and what is above it. Beneath the men in the boat we see the water and the creatures of the water, in this case hippopotamuses. Above them we see the air and the creatures of the air, graceful, long-necked birds, silhouetted against a stylized background of papyrus plants, represented by parallel lines, broken here and there by the fanning shape of the papyrus flower.

These scenes are arranged in horizontal bands, one above the other, and in Plate II-29 we see two more. In the upper frieze, fishermen are pulling in their nets full of

II-25. **Relief from the tomb of Ti at Sakkareh, showing a servant goading asses.** *c.* 2500 B.C.

II-26. Relief from the tomb of Akhty-hotpe near Sakkareh, showing servants quartering an ox.  *c.* 2500 B.C.

II-27. Relief from the tomb of Akhty-hotpe near Sakkareh, showing servants bringing geese and ducks.  *c.* 2500 B.C.

fish, and every fish is carefully depicted, regardless of the law of gravity.  The spirit of Merer-wy-kuy would not be able to dine on a fish that was not clearly shown.  In the lower scene, men are pulling in eel pots at the end of a rope.  The scenes are sepa-rated by a charming frieze of aquatic birds, plants, and flowers.

Not all the pictures from the Old King-dom were in low relief.  The Egyptians painted directly on flat surfaces as well.  The painting of geese from Medum dates

II-28. Relief from the tomb of Merer-wy-kuy near Sakkareh, showing Merer-wy-kuy standing in a boat. *c.* 2400 B.C.

II-29. Relief from the tomb of Merer-wy-kuy near Sakkareh, showing fishermen. *c.* 2400 B.C.

from the twenty-eighth century B.C. (Plate II-30). This vivid work is one of the oldest examples of Egyptian mural painting. As we have seen, Egyptian artists could indulge in greater realism when they portrayed animals, and the painter seems to have observed ducks closely. He has caught the subtle difference in color between the geese's brownish necks and gray- and black-tipped wings, and he has observed the neat arrangement of their feathers. We hardly notice that the colors have neither shade nor highlight, but fill definite spaces within the

sharp, elegant outline. It may have been this very absence of shading in Egyptian painting that led the Egyptians of the Old Kingdom to prefer low relief.

In the reliefs and paintings we have seen, you have probably noticed that most of the figures looked rather like the same person. There was no attempt to individualize the workmen in the tombs of Akhty-hotpe or Merer-wy-kuy. In fact, Egyptian artists tended to *idealize* their figures, presenting to eternity ideally perfect types of men and women: men with broad shoulders, narrow

II-30. **Painting of geese, from the tomb of Itet at Medum.** *c.* 2700 B.C.

hips, and straight features; slender women with huge eyes and thick black hair. And yet in certain instances there were very definite portraits in Egyptian art.

The great majority of Egyptian statues were made for tombs, and their function was to perpetuate not so much the memory, but the very existence of the dead. A statue would be the dwelling for the soul if any harm should come to the mummified body. A sculptor was sometimes actually called "he who keeps alive," and he ranked higher than a painter in the social scale of ancient Egypt. At first, statuary was the prerogative of the king alone, but its use soon spread to all those who could afford the attentions of a sculptor. In these tomb statues, then, we would expect to find true portraits, and we do, too, but not always.

To begin with, sculptors, like painters, followed certain rules of stylization. Figures were always frontal, never twisting; and, like the figures in paintings, they conformed to absolute rules of proportion, according to squares marked out on the block of stone from which they were hewn, regardless of the proportions of the individual they were meant to represent. Standing figures were generally shown with arms at sides, advancing with the left foot forward. The relief statue of King Mycerinus (Plate II-31), wearing the high crown of Upper

II-31. **Green basalt relief statue of King Mycerinus. Fourth Dynasty.**

Egypt, stands between the goddess Hat-hor, who, apart from being the goddess of love and beauty, was the patroness of the royal family of the Fourth Dynasty, and another goddess, protectress of the region of Diospolis Parva. We recognize Hat-hor because she is wearing the horns of a cow and the disk of the moon. All three figures face rigidly forward. This statue was carved in green basalt, one of the hardest and heaviest of stones, which could be polished to a high shine. Such stones as basalt, diorite, granite, or marble might be expected to last throughout eternity, but they were not easy to come by (Plate II-32). Cut from quarries far in the desert they were dragged by human power to the Nile for transportation. Moreover, they were not easy to quarry. And once in the sculptor's shop, in a world that knew nothing of iron or steel, they were difficult to work. And yet it was done, possibly with copper saws and drills—exactly how we do not know. Needless to say, only the king or members of his family could afford statues of such durability. Lesser people had to settle for the softer limestone or sandstone, quarried from the nearby cliffs overlooking the Nile valley itself, and brightly painted. Only details, like eyes, were accented with color in the harder stone works, so that the viewer could enjoy the beauty of the stone surface.

The limestone statue of the early King Djoser himself is badly mutilated (Plate II-33), but we see here the standard, frontal sitting position used by Egyptian sculptors, with one arm clasped across the figure's waist. In the case of the diorite statue of King Chephren, a pyramid builder, the monarch's hands rest peacefully on his knees (Plate II-34).

Let us look more closely at this statue. It is a perfect example of a kind of Egyptian sculpture. More than any other work of

II-32. **Basalt statue of Princess Redyzet. Third Dynasty.**

its time it displays the Egyptian ideal of godlike majesty. Certainly, it is awe-inspiring, and it was meant to be. But to us it may seem hopelessly rigid and lifeless. The anatomy seems true enough: the muscles of the legs, arms, and chest are in roughly the right positions, although they are suggested by flat general planes with little detail. Yet there seems no life in the figure, and the face is almost totally expressionless. Could this be because the *life* of King Chephren was thought to be within his mummy? Was it thought that the statue would take to itself the spirit of the man when necessary, so that the sculptor need not give it a spirit of its own? Yet somehow its very rigidity and lifelessness give us a feeling of eternity. This is not an individual called Chephren caught in some momentary action; this is a perfect man who will live forever. Better yet, this

II-33. Limestone statue of King Djoser. Third Dynasty.

II-34. Diorite statue of King Chephren. Fourth Dynasty.

61

II-35. Head of King Radedef. Fourth Dynasty.

II-36. Alabaster head of King Mycerinus: Fourth Dynasty.

is actually a god, who has always lived, and always will.

But is this a portrait? Did King Chephren have such broad shoulders, such narrow hips, such superb muscles? And beneath the simple cloth *nemset* headdress do we see the actual features of the king? Do we see here true portraits of Chephren's nephew, King Radedef, or of King Mycerinus, or King Woser-kuf (Plates II-35, II-36, and II-37)? Probably not, although there are those who would disagree. The king was, after all, a god, perfect in all ways. He could not be shown to have a wrinkled face with double chins, a misshapen nose or receding jaw, and so his portrait was idealized. The kings of Egypt faced eternity

with almost identical, perfect serenity. So identical, in fact, that they found it quite easy to usurp each others' statues by merely changing the inscribed name. This is one reason, perhaps the most important one, why we know so many of the kings' activities, and yet have so little notion of their characters.

One of the few exceptions is the copper statue of King Pepy I of the Sixth Dynasty (Plate II-38). This is the earliest metal statue which survives from ancient Egypt. The corrosion of the copper, which was hammered into shape and nailed onto a wooden core, obscures the fine modeling, but the inlaid eyes, alert with intelligence, bring the face to life.

II-37. **Granite head of King Woser-kuf.** Fifth Dynasty.

II-38. **Copper statue of King Pepy I.** Sixth Dynasty.

If we look now at the figures of lesser men, we will see many individuals depicted with a realism we cannot doubt. The statue of Ti, whose tomb reliefs we have seen, may be somewhat flattering (Plate II-39), but in the limestone statues of Prince Re-hotep and his wife Nefret (Plate II-40), we see two vividly recognizable people. Re-hotep was enough of an individual, in fact, to wear a moustache. (Most Egyptians were clean-shaven.) Related to King Snefru, founder of the Fourth Dynasty, Re-hotep was a general and a high priest at Heliopolis, then a center of learning and theology. His tomb was at Medum, in a chapel not far from a royal pyramid, and it contained these statues, which were intact when they were found. Perhaps it is the painted skin and inlaid eyes of quartz; in any case, these two figures give one an uncanny sense of immediate reality. We cannot doubt that both are portraits, and that we see before us a handsome young couple looking very much as they must have in the twenty-eighth century B.C. at the very brink of recorded human history.

The figures of Re-hotep and Nefret tell us something of the way the ancient Egyptians dressed, which is a matter worth studying because styles in clothing, as in art, changed little in Egypt. In fact, there was only one noticeable change, and that took place during the Eighteenth Dynasty, more than a millennium after the days of Re-hotep.

II-39. **Limestone statue of Ti. Fifth Dynasty.**

During all this period women, like Nefret, whose name means suitably "The Beautiful," wore a simple tight garment extending from beneath the bosom to the floor, and attached at the shoulders by two wide straps covering the breasts (Plate II-42). Over this garment they might wear, as Nefret does, a shawl covering the shoulders. Here the sculptor has cleverly suggested the form under the fitted cloth. Such clothing was usually white, made colorful by the addition of jewelry, in this case a headband and the elaborate, wide, collar-like necklace of which the Egyptians were so fond. The details of Nefret's necklace are not clearly depicted, but it was probably made of rows of beads of semiprecious stones or faience (a glazed and fired ceramic). Nefret is wearing a thick wig of human hair cut straight across in the Egyptian fashion, and we can see her own hair underneath. As a woman would today, she has covered the separation of real and false hair with a band, which also holds the wig in place. Re-hotep himself wears only a string with an amulet and a white kilt from waist to knees (Plate II-41). This was typical man's dress, and the kilt might be wrapped or folded in any number of ways. If we look at the statues of the kings we will see that, but for their crowns, they are dressed in precisely the same way. Both Re-hotep and Nefret are barefoot, although sandals existed.

There is still another "stock figure" in Egyptian statuary of the Old Kingdom, and that is the "seated scribe." The scribe sits with his legs crossed, pen in hand, a roll of papyrus resting on his knees, ready to take dictation. In Plates II-43 and II-44 we see two seated scribes, both from Sakkareh, both dating from the Fifth Dynasty, and both masterpieces of Egyptian art. Their faces are alert. We cannot doubt that these are the educated, intelligent men of their

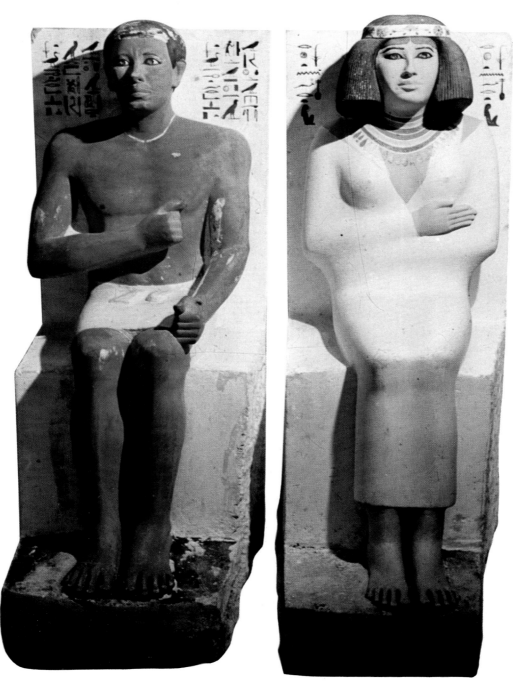

II-40. Limestone statues of Prince Re-hotep and his wife Nefret. Fourth Dynasty.

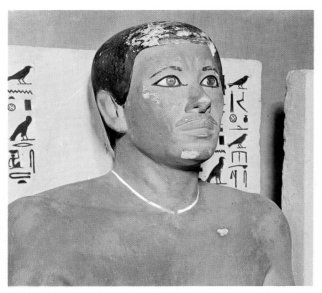 

II-41. **Statue of Re-hotep (detail). Fourth Dynasty.**

II-42. **Statue of Nefret (detail). Fourth Dynasty.**

age. They must both have risen to high office, but it is in their calling as scribes that they are to be remembered. Moreover, we see here two individuals: one lean, high-strung, and taut; the other round-faced, heavyset, and humorous. The second scribe rather resembles the statue of Ranofer (Plate II-45), high priest of the god Ptah, also found at Sakkareh. But even though these are true portraits rather than idealizations, we notice that they are of people in the prime of life, well-built, and with no disfiguring wrinkles or blemishes. They are realistic portraits, but perhaps a bit flattering.

Still, Egyptian portraiture was not always flattering. Egyptian sculptors could portray absolute realism within the bounds of their stylization, even if they rarely did. A figure nicknamed "Sheikh el beled" is a perfect example (Plate II-46). It is actually a statue of an official from Memphis named Kaaper. But when this paunchy figure with sagging chins and belly was dug up, the workmen shouted "Sheikh el beled!"—"the Mayor!" Apparently their local politician had a double in antiquity. "Sheikh el beled" is a veritable masterpiece of unstinting realism. It was carved in wood, and the sculptor paid great attention to the grain of the block with which he was working. The wooden statue of another Memphis official and his wife, dating from the same period, is another example of heavy-featured, brutal

II-43. Limestone statue of a scribe. Fifth Dynasty.

II-44. Limestone statue of a scribe. Fifth Dynasty.

II-45. Head of the statue of Ranofer. Fifth Dynasty.

II-46. "Sheikh el beled." Fifth Dynasty.

realism (Plate II-47). Probably strangest of all is the limestone group of the dwarf Seneb and his wife and family (Plate II-48). The sculptor was perfectly matter-of-fact in depicting the misshapen form of the dwarf. Such treatment of physical defects appears in several statues of the Old Kingdom. If the rarified world of the pharaoh does not come to life before our eyes, that of the commoners beneath him does.

Seneb's wife has tenderly put her arm around the figure of the dwarf. Often in the tomb statues we find couples together this way. Ancient Egyptian family life seems to have been very close. Women and young girls were not hidden away, and women apparently had property rights of their own. Although marriages were often arranged, we cannot doubt that many were for love. The poets wrote:

> When I see her, then will I be well;
> When she opens her eyes, my body
> is reborn.
> When she speaks, I am strong;
> When I embrace her, she banishes evil
> from me.[2]

Many married couples, like Seneb and his wife, faced the other world bravely together.

But if these statues and reliefs were to last forever, strong and well-built tombs were necessary, and the Egyptians were master tomb builders. Building had progressed during the archaic period from the mud hovels and reed shelters of prehistoric days. Important buildings, palaces and temples, like the palace on the stele of King Wadjy Djet, were made of mud-brick and massive structural timbers imported from Phoenicia. The kings equipped

[2] Barbara Mertz, *Red Land, Black Land,* Coward McCann Inc., New York 1966, p. 65

II-48. The dwarf Seneb and his family. Sixth
Dynasty.

II-47. Woodened statue of an official of Memphis and his wife. Fifth Dynasty.

and manned ships to sail to Byblos for cargoes of cedar from the forests of the Lebanon, and the search for permanent materials went on under the Old Kingdom. Wood and mud-brick replaced the lashed bundles of papyrus stalks, rush matting, and palm thatch; and builders began to use stone for lintels, thresholds, and doorposts. Conservative as they were, Egyptian builders often imitated in stone the shapes of the papyrus stalks, the rush matting, and the palm thatch that were no longer in use. Unfortunately, mud-brick and timber do not last, even in Egypt, and it is only through tomb objects, like the sarcophagus of Rawer which is shaped like a house (or palace), that we have some notion of what these buildings were like (Plate II-50). Here we see doors and windows united in a handsome design by long vertical niches. We have only the faintest remnants of Egyptian palaces, and the earliest temples that remain intact date from the Eighteenth Dynasty of the New Kingdom, but we do have many tombs, and temples connected with them, dating from the Old Kingdom. Among them are the most amazing works of Egyptian architecture.

For prehistoric burials the body, lying in a folded position, was buried in a pit along with a few possessions, and a burial mound was placed above it. From this the standard Egyptian tomb evolved. The noblemen of the Old Kingdom whose statues and reliefs we have just seen had "pit and mound" burials also, but of a more elaborate sort. The substructure of the tomb, the "pit," consisted of a whole apartment of brick chambers for the dead buried deep in the ground. Here were rooms not only for the body, but for all the paraphernalia of daily life the deceased was taking with him. Above the "pit," the "mound" consisted of a handsome square structure with slanting,

II-49. **Funerary stele of King Wadji Djet. First Dynasty.**

II-50. **The sarcophagus of Rawer. Old Kingdom.**

70

smooth limestone walls, inset with vertical niches, and having a flat roof. This was the *mastabeh*, and it was here in the mortuary chapel that the living could make contact with the dead. Plate II-51 shows the entrance to the mastabeh of Ti near Sakkareh. The procession of mourners carrying offerings passed through the door into a great hall of pillars, and then into a hall of offerings. The statue of Ti we saw in Plate II-39) stood in a walled-off room called a *sirdab*, but it was allowed to see the display of offerings through a hole high in the wall. Often the chapel had a false door with the deceased carved or painted on it, so that he could step into the realm of the living.

This, then, was the mastabeh, and it remained the standard form of tomb for those who could afford it throughout much of Egyptian history. There were whole cities of mastabehs, with narrow streets between them. Later tombs were cut into the cliffs, and these "rock-cut" tombs retained the same interior arrangements, although the burial chambers were not below, but deep within the rock surfaces. Those who could not afford such tombs were obliged to settle for something simpler, or even for a hole in the ground. It is pathetic that sometimes the poor chose to be buried near the mastabehs of the rich, in hope, no doubt, that their souls would be able to sneak in. But what of the kings, who could afford an even more elaborate burial? At first they, too, were buried in mastabehs, but with King Djoser, founder of the Third Dynasty, Egyptian tomb architecture took another turn.

One of the greatest monuments of the Third Dynasty is the tomb of Djoser at Sakkareh, the great burial ground of the capital of the Old Kingdom at Memphis. This monument, known as the Step

II-51. **Entrance to the mastabeh of Ti, near Sakkareh. Fifth Dynasty.**

Pyramid, was the first pyramid and probably the first stone building in history. It is also a monument to the genius of a great architect, I-em-hotep. The individual sculptors and artists who decorated the tombs were mere craftsmen, and their names have not come down to us. Occasionally we do, however, have the names of individuals responsible for building great monuments, and among these I-em-hotep was the first and most important. Whether he was what we call an architect today we do not know, but he was vizier and "minister of works." The original plan for a tomb for the king that was true to the traditional form of the mastabeh but more imposing than anything yet built must have been

II-52. The Step Pyramid of Djoser at Sakkareh.  *c.* 2800 B.C.

II-53. The enclosing wall and Step Pyramid at Sakkareh.  *c.* 2800 B.C.

II-54. Porch of the Hall of the Columns at Sakkareh.  *c.* 2800 B.C.

conceived by him. In later ages he was celebrated as an astronomer, a priest, and a physician as well as an architect, and was deified as the god of medicine. He might have been considered a mythical figure today had a statue base bearing his name not been found within the very enclosure of the pyramid. We can only wish that we had found the statue itself.

Ancient chronicles claim that I-em-hotep was no less than the inventor of the art of building in stone. And it is true that although there is reference to a stone temple in an inscription from the reign of Djoser's father, I-em-hotep's pyramid is the earliest known stone structure of any great size. Why building in stone developed at this time in Memphis is not hard to imagine. The faces of the valley cliffs provide excellent quarries near at hand.

The actual tomb of Djoser was in a burial chamber constructed of granite slabs brought 700 miles from Aswan, at the bottom of a giant rock pit 80 feet deep sunk beneath the usual square mastabeh. I-em-hotep enlarged the mastabeh by building six superimposed rectangular stages with sloping sides, each smaller in size than the last, reaching upward to a height of 200 feet. He had, in fact, evolved the pyramid by simply piling one mastabeh on top of another. The resulting mound covered an area measuring a staggering 411 feet by 358 feet, and we must imagine it not as the crumbling structure we see in Plate II-52, but faced with smooth white limestone. It may be that the Egyptians saw it as "a gigantic sequence of steps that rise up to the sky, to facilitate the ascent of the deceased to the Sun, Re his father."

This stepped pyramid dominates a complex of buildings surrounded by a huge enclosure wall (Plate II-53). Only one of the fourteen gateways that break the rhythm of bastions and niches in this enclosure wall is a true entrance. Within this enclosure were courts and buildings imitating light structures used at coronations and other ceremonies. These strange buildings are mostly dummies, stone facades that repeat in every detail the facades of buildings of lighter materials, covering cores of rubble. There are stone imitations of wooden doors, some of them barred by imitation stone fences. The great enclosing wall itself, with its recesses and bastions, imitates timber-work, and the splendid fluted columns of the great entrance hall (Plates II-54 and II-55) imitate bundles of reeds or perhaps palm branches. Within the deep burial chambers a pattern of blue-green faience tiles imitates the reed mats with which Egyptian homes were decorated. Everywhere the flimsy world of Egyptian daily life has been translated into the stone of eternity, like some giant fossil.

Within a little over a century, the Egyptians were building stone monuments that have stood the test of time better than any others ever constructed by man—the great pyramids of Gizeh. King Snefru, founder of the Fourth Dynasty, completed the Step Pyramid of Medum we see in Plate II-56 along the lines of the pyramid of Djoser, and this was the last precursor of the true pyramid form. From that time forward, until the end of the Old Kingdom, kings and their queens were buried in tombs with superstructures of pyramid form, on the west bank of the Nile north and south of Memphis. The largest of these were constructed near Gizeh by Snefru's successors, Cheops, Chephren, and Mycerinus, and they were and remain one of the wonders of the world (Plate II-57).

It is easy to see how the pyramid evolved. By smoothing the sides of a stepped pyramid, a form of geometrical per-

II-55.  Hall of the Columns at Sakkareh.  *c.* 2800 B.C.

II-56.  Pyramid of Snefru at Medum.  *c.* 2700 B.C.

II-57. The Great Pyramid of Cheops at Gizeh. 2700–2600 B.C.

II-58. The pyramids of Cheops, Chephren, and Mycerinus at Gizeh. 2700–2600 B.C.

fection was achieved. It has been noticed that when the sun breaks through a cloud in the valley of the Nile, its rays seem to fall at just the angle of the sides of the pyramids, and so they may in some way celebrate the lifegiving rays of the Sun-god, Re. But whatever the reason for the shape, the work that was involved in building the pyramids was staggering. The statistics for the largest, the Great Pyramid of Cheops (Plate II-58), speak for themselves: no less than 2,300,000 limestone blocks were used to build it, most weighing about $2\frac{1}{2}$ and some as much as 15 tons; and the granite slabs which roof the king's chamber (now deep within, rather than beneath the pyramid) weigh nearly 50 tons each. The final pile is some 481 feet tall and measures 755 feet on a side. One might marvel at the work of quarrying such stones, but once out, how were they put in place? We may be truly astounded when we realize that the Egyptians of this period did not have the simplest machines. They did not have the pulley; they did not even have the wheeled vehicle. Scholars have come to the conclusion that there was just one way, one which in this era seems appalling: the stone blocks were floated from quarries across the river at high tide, then dragged to the pyramid and hauled over ramps extending up its side by the force of human muscle alone. The Greek writer Herodotus says that 100,000 men were employed to work on the pyramid, and this is not impossible, although they may not all have worked at once. Egypt was so highly organized that such a number could probably have been mobilized, especially at the time of the year when the rise of the Nile prevented farming.

Most remarkable of all was the accurate dressing of the blocks before they were laid in courses, and in this the skill of Egyptian masons has never been surpassed. The joints between the great blocks of limestone with which the pyramid was faced are no more than a hair's breadth, $\frac{1}{50}$ of an inch,

thick, and that for blocks weighing over 10 tons.

The temples built beside the pyramids were also made of stone throughout and followed the same plan, with an entrance hall, open court, niches for statues, and sanctuary. The temple of Chephren was a rectangular building with two large halls and five chapels. The limestone walls were faced with red granite and the pavement was alabaster. Connected with this mortuary temple by a covered causeway was the smaller valley temple, where purification and embalmment ceremonies took place. It is unusually well preserved, and its granite walls and square pillars are still imposing in their large, simple masses. Its hall with two rows of columns once contained twenty-three royal statues in diorite, schist, and alabaster, including the one of King Chephren in Plate II-34.

II-59. **The sphinx at Gizeh.** *c.* 2700 B.C.

Around the pyramids stood the mastabehs of members of the royal family, but near the valley temple sits one of the strangest configurations ever seen, the great sphinx (Plate II-59). What it is, in fact, is a monumental, 240-foot-long and 66-foot-high figure of a lion with the face of a king, probably Chephren. It was fashioned from a knoll of rock left by the builders when they were quarrying stone for a pyramid core, but this does not detract from its fascination. Why had this mound been transformed into this outsized monster, perched so unexpectedly in the middle of the desert? The answer probably lies in an Egyptian myth that a lion sits guarding the gates of the Underworld, and so it would seem that the king, in the form of a lion, was set down to guard his own tomb. Much has been written about the inscrutable expression on the face of the sphinx, (Plate II-60) but I doubt that, in its undamaged state, when it was probably coated with plaster and painted, it differed very much from the expression of blank and eternal majesty we see on the face of the great diorite statue of Chephren in Plate II-34. But one matter does remain a mystery. The Egyptians, who carefully embalmed and wrapped their corpses, who devoted such effort to every detail in the decoration of elaborate tombs, and who built the great pyramids with their bare hands—were they so very sure of an afterlife? Surely, we feel, they could not have had any doubts. Yet an Egyptian poet wrote:

Cast all evil behind thee and think
  thee of joy—
Until that day comes when harbor is
  reached in the land that loves
  silence.
Spend the day merrily, and weary not
  therein;

II-60. **The sphinx at Gizeh.** *c.* 2700 B.C.

Lo, none can take his goods with him;
  lo, none that has departed can
  come again.[3]

The pyramid of Cheops is the largest, and at no time after him was the single-handed power of the king so great. Pyramids later than the three great monuments were smaller and more poorly built. They paral-

[3] George Steindorff and Keith C. Seele, *When Egypt Ruled the East,* University of Chicago Press, Chicago, 1942, p. 41.

lel the waning power of the king toward the end of the Old Kingdom.

At the time of the fall of the Sixth Dynasty, the might of the pharaoh's central government had been weakened, while landowners who had been granted estates and offices by the king became too powerful. There followed an era we call the First Intermediary Period, a time of disorder, rebellion, violence, and economic chaos. The kings at Memphis had only local authority, and anarchy prevailed in most parts of the country. Land was uncultivated and there was famine. Most of the tombs and temples of the Pyramid Age, with their untold treasures and artistic masterpieces, were systematically pillaged and destroyed. From 2280 to 2060 B.C. one dynasty after another took power, ruling only in name, mere shadows of their great predecessors of the Old Kingdom. Then a new ruling family arose in Thebes in Upper Egypt which triumphed over the feudal princes and provincial nobility who were ruling in their own regions.

Midway through the Eleventh Dynasty, a great king, Montu-hotpe II, reunited Egypt into a single kingdom once more, with Thebes as its capital. The painted limestone statue of him wearing the red crown of Lower Egypt is powerful (Plate II-61), but its massive and crude carving tells something of what happened to the arts during this period. Thebes of the Middle Kingdom never set its stamp on Egyptian art as Memphis had done. The old monuments remained to inspire the new artists and craftsmen of the Eleventh Dynasty, with which the Middle Kingdom began.

When we look at the art of the Middle Kingdom we are struck not so much by a change or development as by a lack of change. The granite head of Amun-em-het II (Plate II-62), the sphinx of Amun-em-het

II-61. **Limestone statue of King Montu-hotpe II.** *c.* 2050 B.C.

II-62. **Granite head of King Amun-em-het II.**
*c.* 2000 B.C.

II-63. **Sphinx of Amun-em-het III. Middle Kingdom.**

II-64. **Statue of Sesostris III.** *c.* 1850 B.C.

III (Plate II-63), and the portrait statue of the great Sesostris III (Plate II-64), all reflect the impassive, changeless grandeur we saw in "portraits" of pharaohs of the Old Kingdom. But the kings here are portrayed according to a new canon: they are not so much deities as sturdy warriors, and occasionally royal faces do show imperfections and age. In the wooden statue of the chancellor Nakhty (Plate II-65), with its lively inlaid eyes we see that the tradition of more realistic portraiture of lesser dignitaries was also upheld. The treatment of low relief, too, remained much the same. The

II-65. Wooden statue of Nakhty. *c.* 2000 B.C.

II-66. Relief of Sesostris I and the god Ptah from the pavilion of Se'n-Wosret at Karnak. *c.* 2000 B.C.

II-67. Relief of Sesostris I and the god Amun from the pavilion of Se'n-Wosret at Karnak. *c.* 2000 B.C.

reliefs in Plates II-66 and II-69 are from the temple pavilion built by Sesostris I at Karnak. In the first we see the king breathing in life from the god Ptah. In all such reliefs people vary in size according to their importance. The king is always much taller than the commoners around him, but as a sign of his rank as god, he is often the same size as other deities. In Plate II-67 he is seen speaking with the god Amun, from whom he claimed descent, and both are identically dressed, wearing the white crown of Upper Egypt. Amun was a Theban god, and with the rise of Thebes to power in the Middle Kingdom, he became State-god

of Egypt, a matter which was later of great importance.

In Plate II-68 we see a tomb object which should be of interest. It is a statue of the *ka* of King Hor. The ka, in Egyptian belief, was thought to be a person's vital force, which accompanied him in life and death. The ka was physically the man's double, although it had a separate existence and acted as the individual's protective genius. In many ways the ka was what we think of as a man's soul, which he rejoined after death, but what we call the soul took several forms to the Egyptians. Besides the ka, there was the *ba,* a human-headed bird seen as living around the tomb and sometimes perched on the chest of the mummy, and the *akh,* a purely spiritual being. This was never depicted, but Egyptians would speak of the akh as we would of "the shades" or "the spirits."

The little statuette in Plate II-69 is the figure of a young girl carrying offerings. She holds a vase in her right hand, while her left arm is raised in a graceful movement to balance the heavy load on her head. The delicately painted embroidery on her tight-fitting dress is particularly appealing. We have seen such servant figures in tombs from the earliest times, but now the little

clay *shawabty*-figures, performing every imaginable task, became popular. There were little clay and wood models of granaries, breweries, tanneries, jewelers' shops, and such, all full of tiny clay figures busily at work, looking more like children's toys than magical assurances of a secure future. In Plate II-70 we see a peasant guiding a plow drawn by two speckled oxen, and in Plate II-71 we see a Nile boat complete with crew, and with a model of the dead man sitting in a cabin on the deck. In such a boat did the deceased expect to make the journey to the kingdom of Osiris.

There are many figures, too, of lovely

II-68. **The *ka* of King Hor.**
Nineteenth century B.C.

II-69. **Statuette of a servant girl.**
*c.* 2000 B.C.

II-70. **Model of a peasant guiding a plow.** Middle Kingdom

blue ceramic dating from the Middle Kingdom. The hippopotamus, an animal which often damaged the crops along the Nile, is here transformed into a lively ornament covered with a bright blue glaze and decorated with the flowers and marsh plants of the river valley. It is interesting that this humorous little figure differs not so very much from the alabaster hippopotamus in Plate II-72 made a thousand years before.

And so, the stream of Egyptian art went on with seemingly little change. And yet there were things in the Middle Kingdom that foreshadowed changes in the future. Traces of fortresses and the first large-scale remains of a city, Kahun, date from this period, and the crowned head of Amun-em-het III (Plate II-73) is surprising in its unflattering realism.

The Middle Kingdom was a time of prosperity and expansion. For the first time Egyptian armies successfully pushed the traditional frontiers of Egypt east into Syria and south into Nubia. But the strong rule

II-71. **Model boat of painted wood.** Middle Kingdom.

II-72. **Blue ceramic hippopotamus. Middle Kingdom.**

II-73. **Crowned head of Amun-em-het III. Middle Kingdom.**

of the kings of the Twelfth Dynasty was not maintained by their successors, and the Middle Kingdom declined from about 1780 B.C. until its fall.

Darkness lies over the Second Intermediary Period in Egyptian history, owing to the lack of historical records, but the absence of large public works, the small size of the few royal tombs, and the disappearance of decorated private tombs suggest a general impoverishment. Moreover, for the first time since the almost mythological unification of the two kingdoms under Nar-mer (or Menes), Egypt was invaded. In the early seventeenth century B.C., bands of a nomadic shepherd people called the Hyksos came from the east and overran the Delta. Little is known about the Hyksos. Some of their names seem to have been Semitic, but no one is quite sure from where they came, or what language they spoke. There were several Hyksos pharaohs, but so conservative were Egyptian artists that it is impossible to tell from their portraits if the Hyksos were in any way different from those who had gone before.

The Hyksos were finally defeated and expelled about 1570 B.C. by a family of princes from Thebes who succeeded in uniting the country. These men founded the great Eighteenth Dynasty of warriors, and with them Egypt moved into a golden age, the New Kingdom.

The Egyptians learned several things from the Hyksos, among them the use of the chariot and the habit, in fact the necessity, of warfare. Their borders were no longer safe as they had been in the time of the Old Kingdom. Thus the Theban princes embarked on military conquests abroad. Under Thut-mose I the Egyptians advanced into Nubia, beyond the third Nile cataract, and occupied Syria as far as the Euphrates. Thebes "of the hundred gates" was the flourishing capital of this new empire, and also the center of the religious and cultural life of the nation. During the next century the west Theban plain was enriched with great temples dedicated to the State-god Amun, and with royal and private tombs.

Strangely enough, one of the most extraordinary rulers of the Eighteenth Dynasty was not a king at all, but rather a queen, Hat-shepsut, daughter of the mighty Thut-mose I. Hers is one of the few genuine characters that emerges from the almost faceless succession of Egyptian pharaohs, and her story is alarming to say the very least.

Although succession to the throne may have followed through the female line, Egypt was ruled traditionally by kings, not queens. Hat-shepsut reigned briefly as queen and wife of her weakling half-brother, Thut-mose II, about whose early death there has been much speculation. Thut-mose and Hat-shepsut did not produce a male heir, however, so succession was to fall to a son of the king by a concubine, Thut-mose III. This boy was less than ten years old when he came to the throne, and his stepmother (and mother-in-law, as he had been married to Hat-shepsut's daughter) took the reins of government as regent, theoretically until he came of age. When that day arrived, however, she was not of a mind to give them up. She had already assumed full power, not as queen but as king. In all reliefs, statues, sphinxes, and inscriptions Hat-shepsut, who described herself as "exceedingly good to look upon, with the form and spirit of a god, . . . a beautiful maiden, fresh, serene of nature, . . . altogether divine,"[4] is seen ruling as an official man. She is shown dressed

only in a white kilt and wearing not only the kingly crown, but also an official false beard.

But for all her eccentricities, Hat-shepsut was an excellent ruler. An official record said "she was a dictator excellent of plans who reassured the two regions by her speaking." Under her firm rule, which lasted from 1489 to 1469 B.C., Egypt was prosperous and secure. She was not interested in military expeditions and encouraged foreign trade in place of conquest. Her commercial expedition to the land of Punt brought ivory and gold, precious woods, incense, spices, and exotic animals into Egypt. Many scholars have tried to guess exactly where this land of Punt was, and it is now thought that it might have been the Somali coast of Africa. Scenes from the expedition are carved in low relief in the queen's mortuary temple at Deir el Bahri.

The construction of this temple (Plate II-74), considered one of the most beautiful in Egypt, was one of the great events of Hat-shepsut's reign. It is always associated with the name of Sen-ne-mut, the queen's chief chancellor, adviser, and closest friend. Like the great I-em-hotep, he was not so much architect as minister of works, and yet the plan for the temple can be attributed to no one else. He exploited to the full the natural grandeur of the site on a rocky hillside backed by rugged cliffs. Here he has raised three colonnaded terraces against the hillside, one above the other, with ramps running up the hill from terrace to terrace. A processional way lined with sphinxes led to the temple, and from the colonnade of the upper terrace a row of huge statues of Hat-shepsut stood against square pillars. In the two lower colonnades the rhythmical repetition of light falling on the columns and the deep darkness of the

---

[4] George Steindorff and Keith C. Seele, *When Egypt Ruled the East,* University of Chicago Press, Chicago, 1942, p. 126

II-74. Funerary temple of Queen Hat-shepsut at Deir el Bahri. Eighteenth Dynasty.

II-75. Square pillars from the chapel of Hat-Hor in the temple of Queen Hat-shepsut at Deir el Bahri. Eighteenth Dynasty.

spaces between was broken only by the central ramps. The square columns (Plate II-75), (one of which bears the head of Hat-hor), statues, and reliefs all had their place in one unified whole. Hat-shepsut herself is depicted everywhere. In the relief in Plate II-76 we see the queen drinking from the udder of the Cow-goddess Hat-hor.

It was not to be expected that Thut-mose III would sit idly by while his stepmother seized his throne, nor did he. Precisely what he did, however, is not exactly clear. After twenty years of rule in name only, he seems to have done away with Senne-mut, and in 1469 Hat-shepsut died, possibly murdered. Thut-mose III then

II-76. Relief of Queen Hat-shepsut drinking from the udder of the Cow-goddess Hat-hor, from Deir el Bahri. Eighteenth Dynasty.

wreaked his vengeance on all that Hat-shepsut had left behind. He set out to destroy every statue and inscription, or obliterate her name and replace it with that of Thut-mose I, II, or III. Thus he hoped to extinguish her life in the next world and to destroy all memory of her in this.

Thut-mose III was one of the greatest conquerors in Egyptian history. In seventeen successful campaigns he extended the frontiers of the empire from the Sudan or Nubia to the borders of Anatolia. He even succeeded in making himself feared by the warlike Assyrians and Babylonians, who sent tribute and offerings of friendship. To commemorate these victories, he had relief sculpture and inscriptions raised at the temple at Karnak dedicated to Amun, or rather Amun-Re, for the State-god and Sun-god were now identified as one.

Thus far, all the temples we have seen have been mortuary temples associated with tombs. It is only from the time of the Eighteenth Dynasty that we have large-scale remains of true temples, centers of the priesthoods, dedicated not to the soul of some departed monarch but specifically to a god or gods. Among the greatest of these was the temple of Amun at Karnak (Plate II-77), parts of which date from the Middle Kingdom. It was at this time that the priesthood of Amun took on great importance in Egypt.

Egyptian temples traditionally followed a set plan that was fairly simple. The earliest were square, flat-roofed buildings entered by a ramp, but all of these have disappeared. By the Eighteenth Dynasty, the Egyptian temple had four basic elements. First there was the gateway or *pylon,* consisting of two towers with sloping sides and flat roofs, flanking the entrance. The pylon must have formed a stunning facade, as it was often covered with brilliantly painted

II-77. **The temple of Amun at Karnak. New Kingdom.**

II-78. **Lotus columns from the temple of Amun at Luxor. New Kingdom.**

reliefs and adorned with colossal statues. In front of it might stand flagpoles bearing standards, or obelisks, tall rectangular shafts topped with small pyramids. These were erected by various pharaohs in honor of the god and symbolized the mountains from which the sun rose. Both flagstaffs and obelisks might be tipped with solid gold. Through the pylon worshipers passed into an open court hemmed by a colonnade or colonnades. Beyond this was the *hypostyle* hall, crowded with a forest of massive columns, needed to support a stone roof. At Karnak, where the hypostyle hall dates from the Nineteenth Dynasty, the stone slabs of the roof rested on impost blocks on top of huge capitals, some, like the one in Plate II-78, so large that a hundred men could stand on top of them. Since these impost blocks could not be seen from below, the roof must have appeared to be floating in air. The effect was enhanced by a "clearstory" arrangement whereby the central section of the roof was higher than the side sections, permitting light to enter. The vast columns that supported this central section were no less than 69 feet high. The "post and lintel" structure, whereby the roof is made of horizontal slabs supported directly by columns, probably originated in the earliest Egyptian buildings, in which reeds and plants were bound together in sheaves to support a covering. As we have seen, the forms of columns and capitals resemble stylized sheaves of papyrus and reeds ending in clusters of buds or open flowers.

The public at large could enter the open court of a temple, but only the privileged few were allowed into the hypostyle hall, and only the pharaoh and priests could enter the sanctuary beyond, which was dark, mysterious and secluded, where the statue of the god stood.

Thut-mose III's descendant, Amun-hotpe II, who ruled from 1436 B.C. to 1411 B.C., built the other great temple dedicated to Amun at Luxor. It was connected to the temple at Karnak by a road flanked by stone rams (Plate II-79). It was at Karnak that the god Amun had his chief sanctuary, but once a year, at the feast of Opet, his great stone image was taken in a solemn procession of boats up the Nile to Luxor. On this holiday there were great celebrations up and down the riverbanks, with free food, music, and a veritable fairground of booths selling mementos. On the river, accompanying the divine boat, which was gilded, ornamented, and decked with flowers, was everything that could float, from the ornate private vessels of the rich to boats full of tourists with minstrels playing as the god went to pay his yearly visit.

II-79. **Avenue of limestone rams leading to temple of Amun at Karnak. New Kingdom.**

II-80. **The courtyard of Ramesses II of the temple of Amun at Luxor, with a statue of the god protecting the king. Nineteenth Dynasty.**

II-81. **Statues between the columns of the courtyard of Ramesses II of the temple of Amun at Luxor. Nineteenth Dynasty.**

Plate II-78 shows the beautiful lotus columns of the colonnaded court at Luxor. A later pharaoh, Ramesses II, added a columned forecourt to the temple (the addition of extra courts and pylons to an already existing temple was a common practice). In Ramesses' court there stands a gigantic statue of the god protecting the king (Plate II-80). Between the columns of this courtyard stand eleven statues of the king (Plate II-81).

The grandiose scale of temple architecture in the New Kingdom required Egyptian sculptors to produce statues in truly huge dimensions. Two vast and battered monumental figures, called the Colossi of Memnon (Plate II-82), are among the most moving works of ancient Egypt, not so much because of their beauty as because of their very desolation. These two seated figures are all that remain of the mortuary temple of Amun-hotpe III. Their size (they are 64 feet high) indicates the scale and grandeur of the vanished building. Its ruins could still be seen in the early nineteenth century, but now the Colossi stand, looking out over the Theban plain, utterly alone.

In statuary of a more manageable size, a notable change came about during the New Kingdom. The white marble statuette of Thut-mose III (Plate II-83) and the red granite statue of Amun-hotpe II (Plate II-84) strike a pose favored by kings of the Eighteenth Dynasty. They are kneeling before the gods with precious offerings. Still, both figures have something of the hard strength of works of the Old Kingdom. This is not true of works like the statue of a young scribe (Plate II-85). If we compare this with the Old Kingdom scribes in Plates II-43 and II-44, we will see that a notable change has taken place. The modeling is softer, the figure altogether

II-82. The Colossi of Memnon. Eighteenth Dynasty.

II-83. Statuette in white marble of Thut-mose III. Eighteenth Dynasty.

II-84. Statue in red granite of Amun-hotpe II. Eighteenth Dynasty.

II-85. **Statue of a young scribe.** Fourteenth century B.C.

II-86. **The sphinx at Memphis.** 1600–1500 B.C.

more relaxed. Or compare the sphinx at Memphis (Plate II-86) with the great sphinx of Gizeh. This smaller work, 15 feet wide by 30 feet long, inspires neither awe nor fascination. This human-headed lion decked with the royal headdress wears an expression of mild serenity. Finally, let us look at the granite group of young Thut-mose IV and his mother (Plate II-87). It was probably made before the king's marriage to a Mitannian princess, while the queen mother held the highest position in the state after the king. Here we see immediately that the surface is far softer than it was in the works of the Old or Middle Kingdoms, and the outline of the figures more blurred. Still, their pose seems rigid, and yet we cannot say that these are true portraits. Little is known of the events of the reign of Thut-mose IV except that the king had the sphinx at Gizeh repaired. The

inscription on the sphinx tells how the king, asleep in its shadow during a hunting expedition, was asked by the Sun-god that the piled-up sand be cleared away from his image.

It was during the Eighteenth Dynasty that painting came into its own. At first tomb reliefs were painted with increasing care and skill, so that color became as important as sculptural effects. A fine example is a painted relief from the shrine to Hat-hor built by Thut-mose III in the Valley of the Kings (Plates II-88, II-89). Here the pharaoh and his chief wife, the "Great Spouse," are seen standing before a pile of offerings. The whole relief is subtly and richly colored. The same richness of color is displayed in the flat painting in Plate II-90 from the same chapel to Hat-hor. This painting gives us a better view of the splendidly rich pattern of color achieved on walls totally covered with paintings of the New Kingdom. Thut-mose III is seen before the seated Amun-Re, pouring a double libation with one hand and holding incense in the other. The god wears a double-plumed headdress and holds the *ankh*, or symbol of life, and a scepter.

The fact was that many of the tombs at Thebes, particularly those built early in the Eighteenth Dynasty, were cut in areas where the rock was not as suitable for relief carving as the stone of Memphis had been. But the stony surfaces of the tomb chambers could be leveled with clay and covered with a layer of plaster as a background for painting. Thus all the shrines and tombs of the Eighteenth Dynasty were decorated with paintings, which were no longer considered

II-87. Granite group of Thut-mose IV and his mother. Eighteenth Dynasty.

II-88. Painted relief from the funerary chapel of Thut-mose III. Eighteenth Dynasty.

II-89. Interior of the funerary chapel of Thut-mose III. Eighteenth Dynasty.

II-90. Detail of a wall painting from the funerary chapel of Thut-mose III. Eighteenth Dynasty.

II-91. **Wall painting of a group of ladies at a party, from the tomb of Neb-Amun. Fifteenth century B.C.**

a cheap substitute for relief decoration.

Most important, as painting developed, the restricting ground line disappeared, and distance could be suggested, while the movements and gestures of figures became far freer, and soft drapery and hair could be more easily portrayed. Scenes of hunting and fishing in the Nile marshes teaming with wild life, or languorous dinner parties with music and dancing to entertain jewel-ladened guests—these are fresh and vivid reflections of life in Egypt's golden age.

Just such a banquet is in progress on the walls of the tomb of one Neb-Amun, an official of the Eighteenth Dynasty (Plate II-91). A group of ladies are seated on ebony chairs beside a table piled with food and wine jars. They are beautiful women with huge eyes, splendidly decked out in gold collars, bracelets, and heavy earrings, which can be seen through their large and elabo-

rately curled wigs. Cones of solid perfume or unguent are fixed on top of their head-dresses, and fresh lotus buds hang over their foreheads. They are dressed in the new styles of the age, with gowns of elaborately pleated linen, so sheer it is almost transparent. In another part of the painting we see two young slave girls, wearing only narrow belts, dancing with graceful gestures very like those of Arab dancers today (Plate II-92). On the left a richly dressed musician accompanies them on the double flute. Such itinerant female musicians seem to have been a common sight in ancient Egypt, and may have been hired for an evening's performance. Most extraordinarily, however, the musician is painted in full face, something unheard of earlier in Egyptian art. On the right we see tall vases full of flowers on stands.

In another painting from the same tomb,

II-92. **Wall painting of slave girls dancing, from the tomb of Neb-Amun. Fifteenth century** B.C.

we see a view of Neb-Amun's garden (Plate II-93). It must have been a charming spot, with palms interspersed with flowering fruit trees around a pool stocked with lotus plants, ducks, and fish. Still, as of old, the artist has not attempted perspective. In order to show *every* tree and *every* fish, he has painted the scene from several angles at once: the pool from above, the fishes and ducks in profile, the trees as if flattened to the ground.

Perhaps the most ravishing of all is the scene of Neb-Amun hunting in the marshes (Plate II-94). He dominates the picture, standing on a papyrus skiff, legs and arms balanced symmetrically as he holds a throwing stick in one hand and live birds for decoys in the other. His beautiful young wife stands behind him, and his little daughter, clinging to her father's leg, picks a papyrus flower. Birds, fishes, plants, butterflies, and hieroglyphic symbols fill

II-93. **Wall painting of a view of Neb-Amun's garden, from the tomb of Neb-Amun. Fifteenth century** B.C.

II-94. **Wall painting of Neb-Amun hunting in the marshes, from the tomb of Neb-Amun. Fifteenth century** B.C.

every corner of the composition. On the left the family cat, gracefully perched on a papyrus plant, wreaks havoc with a covey of birds. (Cats were a favorite house pet in ancient Egypt. Touchingly, the Egyptian word for cat was *miw*.) We can see that Egyptian painters were using different color combinations and learning new techniques

of brushwork, breaking up the surface with fine strokes to suggest feathers, scales, or fur.

All these paintings tell us of the luxury and elegance of society in the New Kingdom, when clothes became more sumptuous, gold more abundant, and pleasures more elaborate than ever before. Yet we must ask ourselves whether Neb-Amun, surrounded by these delights, faced death with the simple faith of the Old Kingdom. In thought and in literature, man had now become more subtle and philosophical. A poet of this golden age wrote of death:

Death is in my mind today
Like the perfume of lotus blossoms,
Like tarrying at the brim of the wine-
    bowl.

Death is in my mind today
Like the clearing of the sky,
As when a man grasps suddenly what
    he has not understood.

Death is in my mind today
Like the longing of a man for his
    home,
When he has passed long years in
    captivity.[5]

The brilliant Eighteenth Dynasty came to an altogether strange end, an end for which nothing that had happened before in Egyptian history could have prepared us.

Scholars had long been mystified by reference to a "heretic king," one held in horror, called "the criminal of Akh-et-Aten," but to what this referred they had no idea. Then one day near the end of the last century, an old peasant woman who was digging on a bank of the Nile for fertilizer came upon some incised clay tablets. These proved to be nothing less than the royal correspondence of a king of the Eighteenth Dynasty. When the site at which they were found was excavated, near the village of Tell el Amarneh, the extraordinary tale of the life of Amun-hotpe IV came to light.

Amun-hotpe IV ruled as co-regent with his father Amun-hotpe III, but this mystic and eccentric young man was devoured by a passion for religious speculation and evolved in his mind a belief in a single god. It may be that he was influenced by the priests of the Sun-god Re-Hor-akhty with whom he studied at Heliopolis, but where he got his notions no one is quite sure.

What is certain, however, is that after the death of his father he made the worship of one god, Aten, the official religion of the state. His religious reform, or heresy, aimed at expressing a single aspect of religion, simple and accessible to all. Instead of Amun, "the Hidden One," whose cult had brought increasing wealth and power to the priesthood, Aten, represented as the disk of the sun, was to be worshiped as the one and only god, the sublime power of the universe.

The temples of the other gods of Egypt, venerated now for two thousand years, were closed, their property seized, and their statues destroyed. The priesthood of Amun particularly suffered. The name of Amun was banned, and all names compounded with Amun were changed. Thus Amun-hotpe IV changed his own name to Akh-en-Aten, "He Who is Beneficent to Aten." The complexities of Egyptian theology and the practice of magic which set the priesthood apart from the people were to be abolished. It may have been that the occult mumbo jumbo of traditional religion could no longer grip the imaginations of the sophisticated and worldly-wise people of the tomb of Neb-Amun. The king now cast it aside in favor of a pure and clear monotheism. He may have written the great

[5] George Steindorff and Keith C. Seele, *When Egypt Ruled the East,* University of Chicago, Chicago, 1942, p. 214

hymn of praise to Aten himself:

> . . . When at dawn thou risest on the
>    horizon and shinest as the orb
>    of day,
> Thou dispellest the darkness and
>    pourest forth thy rays . . .
> Thou hast made the earth according
>    to thy will alone:
> Mankind, cattle, and all other beasts,
>    everything on earth that walketh
>    on feet,
> And everything lifted on their wings
>    in flight,
> The foreign lands of Syria and Kush,
>    and the land of Egypt.
> Thou settest each man in his own
>    place and thou carest for his
>    wants; . . .
> As for every distant land, thou hast
>    provided their living also . . .[6]

Akh-en-Aten wished to free his people
from the ancient traditions and formulas he
felt were stifling them. One of his first
changes was the adoption of the spoken
language for official documents. But most
important was the effect of Akh-en-Aten's
theories on art. The king wanted everything to reflect *ma'et,* the truth. In art
especially the old formulas were to be discarded, and the artist was to portray every-
one and everything exactly as he saw it.

The figures of the king and his wife
Nefret-ity, made early in his reign (Plate
II-95), make clear the beginning of this,
the "Amarnian revolution" in art. The
king is shown with his flabby physique
exactly as it was—he had a pendulous jaw,
heavy hips, and a bulging stomach—rather
than as a broad-shouldered, wasp-waisted
ideal. In the years immediately after his

[6] S. N. Kramer (translator), *Sumerian Mythology,* American Philosophical Society, Philadelphia, 1944

II-95. **Limestone group of Amun-hotpe IV
(Akh-en-Aten) and his wife Nefret-ity. Fourteenth century B.C.**

accession sculptors seem to have been personally instructed by the king to portray him with complete realism.

Akh-en-Aten felt that the new deity should have his own sacred city, and so commenced to build the splendid settlement he called Akh-et-Aten on the great plain of Amarneh between Memphis and Thebes. Here he had built for himself a palace which was the largest private building in the ancient world. Its ruins show it to have been a truly extraordinary succession of halls, courts, gardens, and private apartments, including a great "window of appearance" with a balcony from which the king and his family could salute the crowd.

In one room of the royal residence was discovered a charming painting of two of Akh-en-Aten's daughters (Plate II-96). In many ways we may say that the painter has not solved the problems of representing reality. He still shows no sense of perspective, and rather than foreshorten parts of the body, he has followed the usual rule of profile head and legs with full shoulders. But these figures are more relaxed than anything we have seen before. The girls may have had strangely elongated heads, and this peculiarity has been stressed rather than hidden. Moreover, they appear to be caressing each other affectionately. In fact, Akh-en-Aten, his wife, and six daughters seem to have made a particularly intimate and affectionate family. In the king's house there was no separate queen's apartment as there had always been; Nefret-ity shared the king's own rooms. Now the monarch, before portrayed only stiffly seated or standing, could be seen slouching in a chair, fondling his wife, or kissing his baby daughter. Moreover, the royal family could be seen all over the walls of Akh-et-Aten. Whereas formerly the tombs of noblemen were decorated with scenes of their own life,

II-96. **Wall painting of two of the daughters of Akh-en-Aten from Tell el Amarneh. Fourteenth century** B.C.

they were now decorated with scenes of Akh-en-Aten and his family worshiping or generally enjoying *their* life. This may be because Akh-en-Aten saw himself as the actual incarnation of Aten, whom only he could worship. Others were to worship *him*.

Apart from the palace, the new city contained splendid homes for the king's officials, smaller houses for workers, and a great temple of Aten. This was a new kind of temple, as the new god was to be worshiped in the open air at an altar in the middle of an open court. The fragment of a relief in Plate II-97 shows the king, the queen, and one daughter raising offerings to Aten, seen as the disk of the sun with rays ending in hands that extend toward the king. Some of the hands hold forth the hieroglyphic sign representing life for the king and queen. Akh-en-Aten, with his jutting jaw and sagging belly, is easily identified. He seems almost caricatured. It is possible that the king was in fact suffering from a disfiguring ailment. But now that the king was realistically portrayed, courtiers and lower individuals were no longer. Rather it became stylish to look like the king, and elongated jaws and heads and bulging stomachs are to be seen all over the ruins at Amarneh. The wooden head in Plate II-98 probably formed part of the decoration of a harp, and it, too, is most probably a fair likeness of the monarch.

Still, these exaggerations did not last, and the greatest sculptors of the Amarneh period understood the possibilities of the new realistic approach to art. They took molds of living faces and studied their models, aiming at the closest possible likeness and trying at the same time to convey something of the inner life which animated the face. We can see the result in the head of Nefret-ity by the master sculptor Thutmose (Plate II-99). The name Nefret-ity means "The Beautiful One Has Come," and when we look at this portrait of what must be one of the most exquisite women in history, we see that this is quite literally true. Moreover, Nefret-ity accented her grace by preferring to wear a tall blue crown covering all her hair, of a shape not usually worn by Egyptian queens. The sculptor has shown not only the features but also the structure of bone and muscle, the foundations of a superb beauty. He has, in effect, done virtually overnight what elsewhere it

II-97. **Fragment of a relief showing Akh-en-Aten, Nefret-ity, and a daughter raising offerings to Aten, from Tell el Amarneh. Fourteenth century B.C.**

II-98. **Wooden head from Tell el Amarneh, probably part of the decoration of a harp. Fourteenth century B.C.**

99

II-99. **Head of Queen Nefret-ity, from Tell el Amarneh.  Fourteenth century** B.C.

took centuries to develop.  He has sculpted a figure of anatomical perfection, and moreover one of a beauty so eternal that although the handsome women of the last century or even the last generation may seem dated, Nefret-ity does not.  In addition, he has suggested a mood, expressed in a faint smile, that holds us fascinated with the character of the model.  The quartzite head of Nefret-ity in Plate II-100, although unfinished, shows us the same delicate features and unmistakable tilt of the head, as well as that same enigmatic expression.

The fragment of a statuette in red quartz, probably of Nefret-ity (Plate II-101), and the relief statue of a lady, the wife of the general Nakht-Min (Plate II-102), show the same extraordinary ability and refinement in the sculpting of the body.  Here are translated into stone the delicate fanning drapery of fine linen we saw in the wall paintings of the tomb of Neb-Amun.  Through it we can make out the anatomically perfect contours of the body and the softness of the flesh.  Not again until the golden age of Athens would sculptors be so skilled at portraying the draped human figure.  Everything has been done to give statues of the human form the life and humanity which they had previously lacked.

But events too soon turned against Akh-en-Aten.  At first, Nefret-ity became estranged, for what reason we do not know, and went to live in the north end of the city taking the king's brother Tut-ankh-Aten, then a child, with her.  She seems to have been replaced in Akh-en-Aten's affections by his daughter Merit-Aten and son-in-law (and possibly half-brother) Sem-ankh-kareh, whom he appointed co-regent.  Meanwhile, Akh-en-Aten, who had no use whatever for foreign conquest, seems to have let go of the Egyptian empire so hard-won by his ancestors.  The very correspondence which first led to the discovery of the site of Amarneh shows that the local Egyptian governors in Syria and Phoenicia pleaded for aid from the pharaoh for years on end without receiving it.  In any case, for reasons we do not know, the man who has been called "the first individual in history" died in what was probably his forty-first year, the seventeenth of his reign.  His religious revolution did not survive his death.

Akh-en-Aten's successor and youngest brother, the nine-year-old Tut-ankh-Aten,

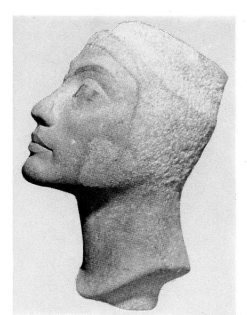

II-100. Quarzite head of Queen Nefret-ity, from Tell el Amarneh. Fourteenth century B.C.

II-102. Relief statue of a lady, the wife of general Nakht-Min. Fourteenth century B.C.

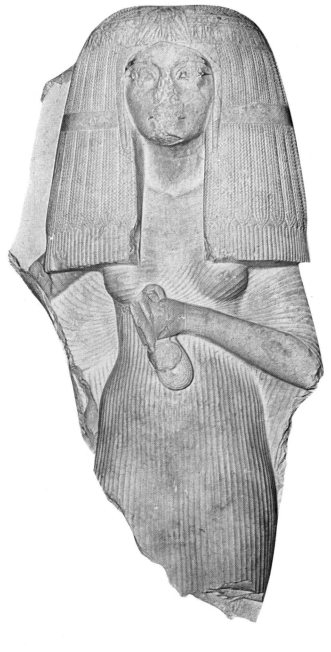

II-101. Statuette in red quartz, probably of Nefret-ity. Fourteenth century B.C.

was completely in the power of Ay, his vizier, and Hor-em-heb, the commander-in-chief of the army. The capital was moved back to Thebes, and willingly or under compulsion the young king restored the official cult of Amun and changed his name to Tut-ankh-Amun. The priests reasserted their authority; and Akh-et-Aten was abandoned and destroyed, its sculpture and paintings defaced and all traces of the heretic king and queen removed. In his haste, or perhaps no longer caring, the sculptor Thut-mose left the head of Nefret-ity, among other works, in his abandoned studio.

The boy-king Tut-ankh-Amun ruled until his death only nine years later, and his reign would have been insignificant had he not, by the merest chance of fate, become the most famous of all Egyptian pharaohs. The reason for this goes back some generations, to the time when the early pharaohs of the Eighteenth Dynasty concluded that a tomb of outstanding size and magnificence defeated its own purpose. It was sure to attract tomb robbers, as had those of almost all earlier pharaohs, and as a result the soul of the deceased would be obliged to face eternity no better equipped than a beggar. Worse still, in an effort to destroy the vengeful spirits of the robbed dead, the robbers often went so far as to mutilate the corpse itself. And so the kings built their "rock-cut" tombs hidden away in the cliff face of a valley on the west bank of the Nile near Thebes. The entrances to these tombs were to be as secret and as inaccessible as possible, and the mortuary temples were no longer built near the tombs themselves, but miles away at the edge of the cultivated land. Still and all, no tomb can be totally secret, as the workmen who built it would know its location, and so sooner or later every tomb in this Valley of the

Kings, at least every one thus far found, was plundered, with one exception. The entrance to the small, hastily thrown together tomb of the young King Tut-ankh-Amun was somehow blocked by the hut of laborers working on the tomb of another king, and eventually forgotten. So it was that when it was discovered by a group of archeologists led by Howard Carter in 1922, it was almost untouched, the only complete royal burial ever discovered. In place of the usually bare walls, trinkets, and statues to be found in most tombs long since rifled, Carter and his team found themselves surrounded by a golden treasure of a value past all reckoning. This was the wealth that was to accompany the incarnation of an Egyptian god through a golden eternity.

The body itself was well protected. Over the red sandstone sarcophagus were four square, gilt wooden shrines, one within another. The second was covered with a linen veil spotted with gilt daisies. Moreover, within the richly carved sarcophagus were three coffins, again resting one within another, in the fashion of Chinese boxes, all in the form of the mummy itself. The outer coffin of gilt wood and gold leaf gave way to the second coffin, made of wood covered with hammered gold inlaid with brilliantly colored glass, paste, and lapis lazuli (Plate II-103). The king's arms are crossed on his chest, and he carries the insignia of Osiris, the scepter and flail. The superb workmanship can be seen if we look at the base of this coffin (Plate II-104). Here, engraved in the gold lining, we see the goddess Isis, unfolding her plumed wings to protect the king. Within this coffin rests still a third coffin, this one of solid gold (Plate II-105). Weighing over 2,448 pounds, it is finely engraved and studded with carnelian, turquoise, and lapis lazuli. When this was finally opened, the

II-103. Middle coffin of King Tut-ankh-Amun. Eighteenth Dynasty.

II-104. Gold base of the middle coffin of King Tut-ankh-Amun. Eighteenth Dynasty.

discoverers of the tomb were astounded to find, resting on the mummy itself, a splendid solid gold mask of great artistry. As were the faces of all the inner coffins, the mask was a vivid, lifelike portrait of Tut-ankh-Amun (Plate II-106). His boyish features were not unlike those of Akh-en-Aten, and they are portrayed in the realistic style of the art of Amarneh.

Within its many layers of linen wrapping, the body of the young king was covered with golden earrings, pendants, pectorals, bracelets, rings, and every imaginable form of jewelry, all of the most exquisite

II-105. Detail of the inner coffin of King Tut-ankh-Amun. Eighteenth Dynasty.

workmanship. Gold was everywhere. The burial chamber and the adjoining rooms contained gold statues, jewelry and jewel boxes, gold ornaments of every type, and chests inlaid with ivory and ebony, presided over by a strange, black, painted statue of the jackal-headed Anubis, the Embalmer-god. The gold statuettes of the goddess Sakhmet with the head of a lioness crowned by the solar disk, and the god Ptah, her consort, give us some idea of the strange enchantment of these gold pieces (Plate II-107). The object in Plate II-108 was a shrine of gilded wood, nearly 2 feet high, which originally contained a solid gold statue of Tut-ankh-Amun. The reliefs on the side panels and doors represent scenes in the life of the young king and his wife, Queen Ankhes-en-Amun, the daughter of Akh-en-Aten. These, too, were executed in the style of the school of Amarneh.

Apart from objects made of precious metals and jewels, there were superb clothing, robes heavily embroidered with intricate beaded patterns, and other fine textiles. In Plate II-109 we see a fragment of cloth painted with figures that appear to be Negro and Syrian prisoners with bows placed upright between them. The more

II-106. **Gold mask of King Tut-ankh-Amun. Eighteenth Dynasty.**

II-107. **Gold statuettes of the goddess Sakhmet and the god Ptah, from the tomb of Tut-ankh-Amun. Eighteenth Dynasty.**

II-108. **Shrine of gilded wood from the tomb of Tut-ankh-Amun. Eighteenth Dynasty.**

II-109. **Fragment of cloth from the tomb of Tut-ankh-Amun. Eighteenth Dynasty.**

fragile possessions, such as these, were stored in superbly painted wooden boxes like the one in Plate II-110. On it we see the king, shown on a larger scale than the other figures, standing alone in his chariot, the reins tied around his waist (an unlikely trick for a king to try), while shooting at Syrians and Nubians who flee in confusion.

Perhaps most interesting of all were the pieces of furniture that accompanied Tut-ankh-Amun to his last rest. Egyptian furniture was of excellent design, lean and elegant. The tomb contained such ingenious pieces as a three-part folding campaign bed. The chair in Plate II-111, intricately inlaid with precious stones set in sheet gold, combines the backrest of an ordinary chair with a curved seat imitating the

sag of a cowhide camp stool. Its crossed legs are not shown. This seat was probably used during religious ceremonies, and it is interesting that this type of chair was the model from which the episcopal thrones of the Christian church were later adapted. In Plate II-112 we see the back of a cedarwood chair, decorated with awe-inspiring Egyptian symbolism. In the center is the Spirit of Eternity who holds in his hands reed shoots (evoking years without number) resting on tadpoles, signifying "hundred thousand." The winged disk of the sun dominates the scene from above.

But the most ornate of all the objects in Tut-ankh-Amun's tomb is the superb throne (Plates II-113 and II-114). It is carved in wood, lined with gold, and inlaid with

II-110. Wooden box painted with scenes of warfare, from the tomb of Tut-ankh-Amun. Eighteenth Dynasty.

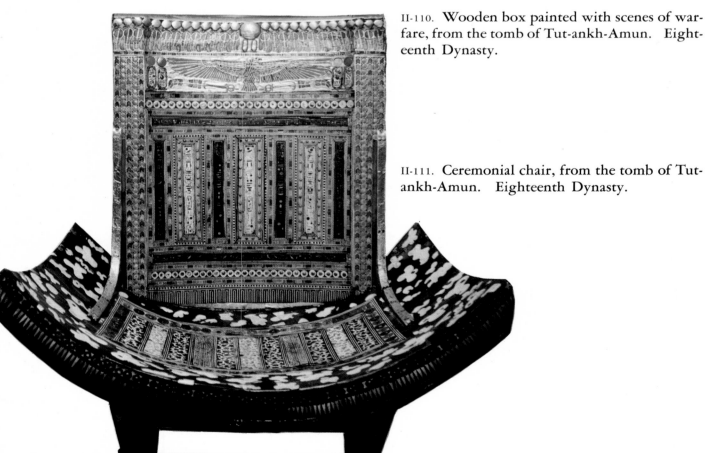

II-111. Ceremonial chair, from the tomb of Tut-ankh-Amun. Eighteenth Dynasty.

106

II-112. **Back of a cedarwood chair from the tomb of Tut-ankh-Amun. Eighteenth Dynasty.**

silver, glazed ceramic, multi-colored glass, paste, and semi-precious stones. The legs are strengthened by open-work carving of which only the central elements have survived. Originally they were intertwined lily and papyrus plants, symbolizing the union of the two lands. The scene which decorates the back of the throne is worked in sheets of gold and silver, colored glass, paste, and glazed ceramic, and it is this which makes the throne more than merely an elaborate piece of furniture. The pretty young queen, who resembles her mother, is shown tenderly anointing her husband's jeweled collar with a perfumed unguent. Like the monarch of Amarneh, the king slouches back in his chair, and the whole scene has the soft freedom, intimacy, and natural grace of the works of the Amarneh artists. Moreover, and this is truly puzzling, we see the solar disk of Aten shedding

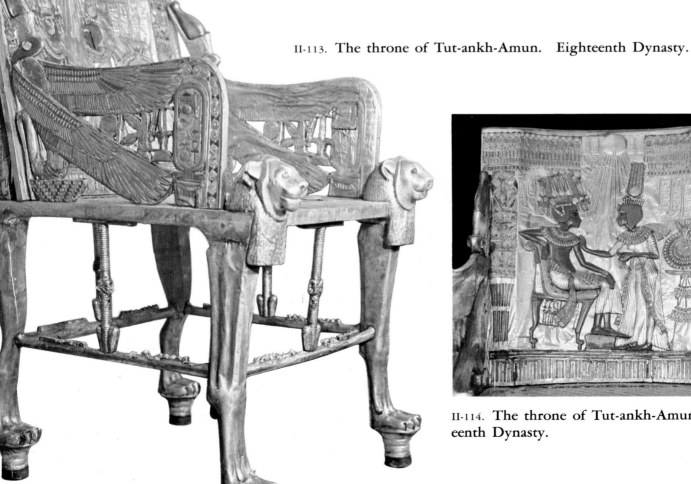

II-113. **The throne of Tut-ankh-Amun. Eighteenth Dynasty.**

II-114. **The throne of Tut-ankh-Amun. Eighteenth Dynasty.**

its rays on the young couple. We may assume, in any case, that even if the king of Amarneh were dead, his artists were not. Their work is still to be found in the tomb of Tut-ankh-Amun.

What became of the charming young queen after the death of her husband? The records of the Egyptians do not tell us, but the records of their enemies, the Hittites, give us some information. Twice the young Queen Ankhes-en-Amun, daughter of Akh-en-Aten, urgently wrote to the king of the Hittites asking that he send one of his many sons to marry her and become pharaoh of Egypt (we must remember the succession probably followed the female line). But her efforts were to no avail. The Hittite prince was murdered on his way to Egypt, and after the short reign of the vizier Ay, power was seized by Hor-em-heb, commander-in-chief of the army, and the brilliant Eighteenth Dynasty came to an end. Whatever finally became of Ankhes-en-Amun is unknown.

The last great creative epoch of Egyptian culture was the Eighteenth Dynasty. During the next two dynasties (1304–1080 B.C.), which brought the New Kingdom to an end, art returned to its traditional conservatism in reaction to the Amarneh revolution. Hor-em-heb's own tomb in Thebes was decorated with the flat and posed stylization that had characterized Egyptian art for two millennia (Plate II-115). His vizier and commander-in-chief, Pa-Ramesses, became king as Ramesses I and founded the Nineteenth Dynasty. He was succeeded by Sethy I and Ramesses II, both efficient rulers, successful soldiers, and active in building temples and monuments. Sethy I recovered many of Egypt's dominions in Syria and Palestine which had been lost in Akh-en-Aten's reign. He and his more famous son, Ramesses II, met the challenge of the greatest neighboring power, the Hittites, at Kadesh on the Orontes in Syria. This battle, commemorated over and over again in temple reliefs, really ended in a draw and led to a treaty between the Egyptian and Hittite empires which gave fifty years of peace to the area. A new capital was established at Tanis in the eastern Delta, from which the reconquered

II-115. **Fresco from the tomb of Hor-em-heb in the Valley of the Kings, Thebes. Eighteenth Dynasty.**

II-116. **Facade of the temple at Abu Simbel. Nineteenth Dynasty.**

Mediterranean lands could be governed more easily than from Thebes. But Thebes remained the religious and cultural center of Egyptian life, and the royal tombs were still quarried out of the rocks in the Valley of the Kings.

It has been said that if the greatness of an Egyptian pharaoh were measured by the size and number of monuments remaining to perpetuate his memory, Ramesses II would be the equal if not the superior of the proudest pyramid builders. The length of his reign, sixty-seven years, the number of his children, the massive bulk of monuments bearing his name built a legend around him; and he has left a tremendous shadow across ancient Egyptian history.

Ramesses' monuments are more impressive for their size than for their artistic quality. He and Sethy I were responsible for a huge hypostyle hall at Karnak with a ceiling 79 feet high, but even its vast scale did not relieve the sense of constraint and heaviness produced by the silent forest of columns, every inch of which are covered with decorative relief.

The most ambitious of all Ramesses II's monuments is the great temple of Abu Simbel, cut out of the rocky cliffs overlooking the Nile in the Sudan, north of the second cataract. The temple, carved out of solid rock, is majestically impressive, but it is essentially a vast facade with little functional space behind it. The basic temple plan has been preserved, with the rock face we see in Plate II-116 serving as pylon.

In one sense Abu Simbel is the culminating point in the development of one theme in Egyptian art: the god-like character of the pharaoh. The four colossal statues of the king against their rugged background are imposing through sheer size. They are no less than 65 feet high, actually larger than the Colossi of Memnon. But they are static, with none of the dynamic power and controlled energy of the royal statues of the Old and Middle Kingdoms. At a period when sculptors had learned to reproduce the bone construction of a face and folds of a dress with the utmost skill and precision, the legs of the statues at Abu Simbel are coarsely carved, as shapeless pillars with no trace of muscular plasticity. Less than ten years ago, the temple of Abu Simbel and the surrounding area would have been flooded by the crea-

II-117. **Head of a statue of Ramesses II. Nineteenth Dynasty.**

II-118. **Wooden statue of an unknown god. New Kingdom.**

tion of the Aswan dam, but in a daring feat of engineering and with the financial support of fifty-two nations, the entire facade was lifted 200 feet to a position above the level of the water.

In sculpture in the round all traces of the naturalism of Amarneh disappeared, and royal portraits returned to the tradition of Thut-mose III. The fine statue of Ramesses II, shown in Plate II-117, is a good example. It has the calm serenity of the earlier godkings, but power and tension are lacking. Instead there is refinement of detail in the folds of the robe and the pattern of the

crown. Like the emperors of Rome, Ramesses had statues of himself, such as the figure of the pharaoh and the god Ptah in Plate II-119, erected in every city in Egypt. Meanwhile, small figures like the mysterious unknown god in Plate II-118 were, as ever, included in the equipment of the dead, and were, modeled with artistry.

Relief sculpture was changing, from the traditional raised relief used in the beautiful wall decoration of Sethy I's tomb (Plate III-121) and in the powerful figure of the god Har-shuf "with the dread countenance" (Plate II-120), to sunk relief, more deeply

II-119. Limestone group of Ramesses II and the god Ptah. Nineteenth Dynasty.

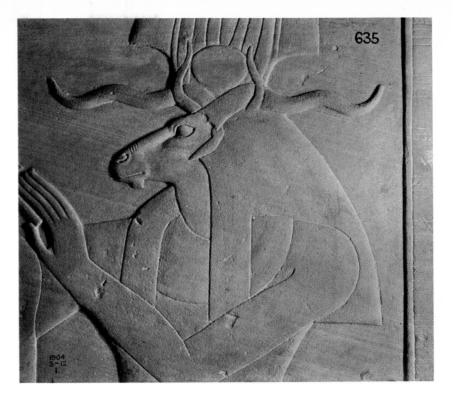

II-120. Sandstone relief of the god Har-shuf. New Kingdom.

II-121. Painted relief from the tomb of Sethy I, Valley of the Kings. Nineteenth Dynasty.

cut and with more swelling surfaces. The latter style is coarser but effective. An example of this is the relief from the tomb of Ramesses VI in Plate II-123.

Yet the changes in relief and painting were not so much in technique as in spirit. From the Fourth Dynasty onward, the paintings and painted reliefs in tombs had depicted scenes from happy and successful lives. The pictures of harvesting, herding animals, hunting, and feasting certainly had a religious or magical purpose, that of helping the dead to achieve a blessed future life. But the emphasis was on life and the denial that death was absolute and meant total annihilation. Then, late in the twelfth century, paintings of funerary rites and the experiences of the dead began to fill all the wall spaces of the tombs, rather than just the burial chambers as before. The Opening of the Mouth Ceremony, the judgment before Osiris, the journey through the Underworld, all show a growing absorption with life after death.

At this time papyri containing magical formulas and instructions for the dead to put to use in the afterlife, often called the Book of the Dead, became popular. In Plate II-122 we see an illustration from such a papyri of the important rite of Opening the Mouth. It is painted on paper made, according to an age-old process, of the pulp of the papyrus plant. The mummy of the dead man is seen supported by the jackal-headed god Anubis, while the priest of Sem in his leopard skin prepares for the ritual of touching the corpse with special instruments to restore the dead man's senses in his future life. This ceremony was always performed on a mummy before its interment, after which it was prepared to join the mourners in a feast. The sunken relief from the tomb of Ramesses VI is a perfect example of a page from such a Book of the Dead translated onto the stone of a tomb wall.

In Plate II-124 we see, from the ceiling of the same tomb, another favorite mortuary

II-122. **Illustration of the ceremony of Opening the Mouth, from the Book of the Dead. New Kingdom.**

scene, the nightly journey of the Sun-god through the Underworld. This scene is strikingly framed by the form of Nut, the Sky-goddess, whose body and outstretched arms form the arched ceiling of the world. In Plate II-125 from the tomb of Sethy I, we see him accompanying the Sun-god on this terrifying trip. The figure of Horus, holding the sign of life, is seen standing in his boat before a gate guarded by a snake which is arched menacingly over the portal through which the sun must pass on his way back to the earth.

When the spirit of the dead man had completed such a tortuous journey—safely, if he carefully obeyed the Book of the Dead and repeated the spells written on the walls of his tomb—he was brought by Anubis for final judgment before Osiris and forty-two judges in the Hall of Double Justice. In another illustration we see the final terrifying ceremony (Plate II-126). Anubis and Ma'et, the goddess of truth, are beside a scale on which the heart of the deceased will be weighed against the symbol of truth—a feather. If the heart is as light as truth itself, Osiris will say, "Let the deceased depart victorious. Let him go wherever he wishes, to mingle freely with the gods and the spirits of the dead."

Painting was much in demand, and the amount of work done led to greater boldness, but less care. Thick black outlines and harsh, crude colors were often used. Yet there are a few genuinely interesting and beautiful murals of the Ramesside period, as, for instance, those in the burial chamber of Sen-nedjem at Deir el Medineh. In Plate II-127, we see the soul pass by boat through the Underworld to the Fields of Yaru, where an idyllic, pastoral life awaits it. It has a sunset color. Another detail shows Sen-nedjem and his wife together in their future life Plate II-128.

II-123. **Sunk relief from the tomb of Ramesses VI. Nineteenth Dynasty.**

II-125. **Painting of the sun's night journey through the Underworld, from the tomb of Sethy I. New Kingdom, fourteenth century B.C. (page 114–115)**

II-124. Painting from the tomb of Ramesses VI, of the journey of the Sun-god through the Underworld, Valley of the Kings. Nineteenth Dynasty.

II-126. Illustration of the weighing of souls, from the Book of the Dead. New Kingdom.

II-127. Painting of the soul passing through the Underworld, from the tomb of Sen-nedjem at Deir el Medineh. New Kingdom.

II-128. Painting of Sen-nedjem and his wife, from the tomb of Sen-nedjem at Deir el Medineh. New Kingdom.

Between 1400 B.C. and 1100 B.C. the balance of power was changing in the ancient Near East. Indo-European peoples from the northeast were seeking homes in the coastal regions of the eastern Mediterranean. The Egyptians called them "the northerners in their islands"; historians call them the sea peoples.

In 1400 B.C. Egypt possessed her empire, with the Hittites emerging as her chief rival. By 1100 B.C. the Egyptians and Hittite empires were destroyed. Assyria was moving east to profit from the wreckage, Israelites and Philistines were in Palestine, the Phoenician city-states were growing in power, the Greeks were established in the Aegean, and iron had replaced bronze as a basic metal. Egypt was again confined to the Nile.

The change from bronze to iron, which Egypt did not possess, led to serious difficulties at home once she was cut off from Hittite territory with its iron and silver. Grain prices soared, dishonesty and factionalism among government officials grew, and the workmen who quarried and maintained the Theban tombs went on strike because the state could not pay them. Robbery and looting from the Theban tombs, rich in gold and silver, were a result of poverty and inflation. This went on for at least a generation, unchecked by responsible officials. The satirical papyri throw an interesting light on this uneasy time. The pharaoh, charging the enemy, is caricatured in battles between cats and mice. Even the gods are treated as objects of farce. However, the temples were wealthier than ever before, enriched by huge bequests of property and cattle from the kings, and dues and taxes in grain and silver. The powerful high priest of Amun had his figure carved on the same scale as Ramesses IX, against all tradition.

When the last Ramesside pharaoh died, Egypt was divided. Thereafter the tale of her long slow decay is a confusing one. About 950 B.C. Egypt was reunited by Libyan princes, who founded the Twenty-second Dynasty with its capital at Bubastis. But civil war soon broke out, and Egypt became a series of independent states until the Kushite or Ethiopian King Piankhy invaded and conquered Egypt in 730 B.C. Kushite rule continued until the Assyrian King Ashurbanipal finally invaded Egypt and sacked Thebes in 663 B.C. Soon the Assyrian empire was broken up, and Psamtik I of Sai in the western Delta regained independence in the north.

During all this period, Egyptian artists continued to repeat, seemingly endlessly, the patterns and formulas of traditional Egyptian art. The statue of the lion-headed goddess of fire, Sakhmet, in Plate II-129, is over life-size and has something of a former grandeur. Competent sunken reliefs, like those of King Osorkon II and his wife (Plate II-130), became more and more common. Moreover, a degree of excellent workmanship was maintained. We can see this is true if we look at the fine ninth century gold pendant of Osiris tightly swathed as a mummy, flanked by Isis wearing the sun disk, and their son Horus the Hawk-god (Plate II-131). The bronze statue of Queen Karomama, of the same period, is superbly inlaid with patterns of gold, silver, and electrum (Plate II-132).

Under the energetic Kushite and Saite rulers Egyptian art actually underwent a revival. Egyptian artists turned passionately to the forms of the Pyramid Age and the Middle and New Kingdoms. This was to be the last resurgence of the Egyptian spirit. The statue of the god Horus in Plate II-133 displays the strength and limitations of sculpture during this last desperate re-

II-129. Statue of the goddess Sakhmet. Late period, tenth century B.C.

II-130. Relief of Osorkon II and his wife. Late period, eighth century B.C.

vival. The hawk-headed god is seen making a purificatory gesture toward a pharaoh. The sculptor has succeeded in imitating Old Kingdom statuary with technical competence, and the modeling of the torso and muscular limbs is masterly. Yet the work as a whole does not evoke the powerful Hawk-god.

In royal statues of the era, like the basalt torso of a pharaoh in Plate II-134, the artists tried to reproduce the timeless serenity of the Old Kingdom, but its essential quality eluded them, as we will see immediately if we compare this work with the immovable strength of the seated figure of King Chephren in Plate II-34.

The standing statue of Mentuemhat, governor of the province of Thebes, as a young man, and the head of the same Mentuemhat when older (Plates II-135 and II-136) are outstanding works of this period. The expressive force and solidity of these portraits recall the statues of earlier times, but now it is the confidence of the

II-132. Bronze statuette of Queen Karomama. Late period, ninth century B.C.

II-131. Pendant in gold and lapis lazuli.
Late period, ninth century B.C.

II-133. Statue of the god Horus. Late period, seventh to sixth centuries B.C.

II-134. Basalt torso of a royal statue. Late period, eighth to seventh centuries B.C.

120

II-136. Head and shoulders of Metuemhat as an older man. Late period, seventh century B.C.

II-135. Granite statue of Metuemhat as a younger man. Late period, seventh century B.C.

models, not the artists, that is lost. We see faces portrayed with the sure realism Egyptian artists were somehow always able to capture, even when most manacled by a stylized form. But these are portraits of a hard man with no illusions living through the last years of a long civilization.

In spite of their sophistication and diligent study of ancient models, and in spite of their mastery of the hardest materials, most of these artists produced statues without life or tension. The same mannered emptiness of spirit is seen in both private statues with their highly polished surfaces

and set smiles, and in the countless figures of deities in bronze, basalt, and serpentine. They are triumphs of technical skill in which stylization of expression and gesture kill any emotion.

This artistic revival ended with the Persian conquest of Egypt in 525 B.C. The Persian rulers claimed to be legitimate pharaohs descended from the Egyptian gods, although Egypt was only a province of their vast empire. Darius I, a wise ruler and lawgiver, built a new temple of Amun on the oasis of Kharga.

The Persian domination of Egypt had no

II-138. Entrance hall of the temple of Kom Ombo. Ptolemaic period.

effect on traditional culture. It was not until the conquest of Egypt by Alexander the Great, welcomed by many as a deliverance, that the foreign influence of highly developed Greek art from the Hellenistic world began to be felt. The funeral mask in Plate II-137, dating from the rule of the Greek Ptolemies, will have a disconcerting effect on our eyes, now familiar with 3,000 years of Egyptian art. The form is traditional, as is the very use of the burial mask. The Egyptian gods are depicted in the rich funeral headdress and gold pectoral, but the face that stares out from the mask is a Greek face proportioned according to the rules and tradition of Greek sculpture. As in many Egyptian works, the face is idealized, but it achieves a Greek ideal. In the temple of Kom Ombo, built near the Nubian border by the Ptolemies (Plate II-138), we see a strangely mixed vegetation, with the acanthus capital of the Greeks among the papyrus and lotus capitals native to Egypt.

But in a detail of a column from Kom Ombo (Plate II-139), we see the Egyptians maintaining their conventions to the bitter end. Moreover, the head of an unidentified pharaoh of the fourth century (Plate II-140) shows that, to the very last, Egyptian artists were capable of works of strength and genius. The bronze figures of the Cat-goddess, Bastet, from the Roman period itself (Plate II-141), shows the ageless scorn of an ancient civilization. But the vital force of Egyptian art was dead, and by Roman times the country, except for Alexandria, was a provincial backwater: "The bright day is done, and we are for the dark."

Looking at figures of gods and pharaohs of the late period, we have noticed how they differed from earlier works, but these are

II-139. Detail of a column, from the temple of Kom Ombo. Ptolemaic period.

II-140. **Head of an unidentified pharaoh.** Late period, fourth century B.C.

II-141. **Bronze statuette of the Cat-goddess Bastet.** Roman period, first century B.C.

fine, subtle gradations. What is more remarkable is how closely they resemble works of the Old Kingdom—how little, not how much Egyptian art changed over a period of three millennia. It is rather as if we were to try to imagine what it would be like if our ancestors at the time of, say, Homer, dressed themselves as we do, lived in the same houses, and drove the same cars. And yet the Egyptians had, as we do, a sense of history and the passage of time. Sightseeing was a favorite occupation, and when

tourists of the time of the Ptolemies went to see the great pyramids of Gizeh, they were viewing monuments as old to them as the Acropolis at Athens is to us. But the lack of alteration would not have surprised them. Swift change is, in fact, a comparatively modern idea. The Egyptians had never known it and did not expect it. Rather they expected the tombs which had endured a seeming eternity before their birth to endure an eternity after their death.

WHERE WAS WESTERN civilization born? In the valley of the Nile or the plain between the Tigris and the Euphrates? Scholars differ in their opinions, and no one can say for sure. But what is certain is that 800 miles to the east of the Nile, on the other side of that impenetrable desert that protected Egypt for so long, another civilization was developing at the very time that the Egyptians first built their canals and their pyramids.

If we look at the map in Plate III-1, we will see that the Tigris and Euphrates both empty into the Persian Gulf, and that a great fertile plain stretches between and around these rivers. This plain is called Mesopotamia, meaning "the land between the rivers." Here conditions were very like those we have seen in Egypt. In this case two great rivers flooded the plain regularly, bearing water and fertile silt to the fields. But there were differences in the kind of flooding, and these marked Mesopotamian civilization deeply. For one thing, the flood was not confined by high cliffs, such as overhung the valley of the Nile. Instead, the waters could rush freely over the surrounding plain obliterating everything, after which the rivers might retreat to different beds, altering their courses. Moreover, the rivers did not flood at the same time each year, nor at a time convenient for farming, and the water had to be stored. To control these inundations, higher levees and a more complicated system of canals were needed. The legend of a flood, in which an angry god saw all of humanity swallowed up, had its origin here. Nor did Mesopotamia rest safely behind a barrier of sands, as Egypt

III-1. **Map of the principal centers of Mesopotamian civilization.**

did. To the north were fertile hills with rainfall and vegetation much like that we know in Europe and America today, and the valley was open to invasion from several directions. As we shall see, onslaughts by bands of marauders were a common thing throughout Mesopotamian history.

The Bronze Age developments—the plow and the potter's wheel, the loom and the art of spinning, the casting and working of bronze—came sooner to Mesopotamia than they did to Egypt. Moreover, the wheeled vehicle, not yet used in Egypt, was known here. By the third millennium B.C., a civilization as rich, complicated, and fasci-

125

III-2. Ruins of the Sumerian city of Ur, third millennium B.C.

nating as that of Egypt had developed in ~~the valley of the two rivers~~

mountains themselves.  These man-made ~~towers could be seen by every inhabitant.~~

III-4. **Tumbler, from Susa.**  *c.* 3100 B.C.

III-3. **Open bowl, from Susa.**  Fourth millennium B.C.

geometrical patterns which derived from natural forms but became gradually more abstract.  The clay figure of a women worshiper (Plate III-5) is older still and appears crude when compared with later work. It goes back, in fact, to 3800 B.C.  If we look closely, we will notice the type of clothing Sumerian women of this period wore, a sheepskin garment like a shift and a sort of turban.  Like so much of Mesopotamian art, it was inspired by the all-important religion of the great valley.

The Sumerians were a profoundly religious people with a large pantheon of gods.  Most of these, such as Anu the Sky-god, Sin the Moon-god, and Ishtar the goddess of fertility, were worshiped everywhere, but each city had its own divine patron or protector living in the most important temple.

III-5. **Clay statue of a woman worshiper, Mesopotamia.** *c.* 3800 B.C.

The gods, formidable and jealous of their rights, were feared rather than loved, except the mother goddess of the earth, who interceded with the others to take pity on human beings. Yet the gods were very close to men. Their houses, the temples, stood in the midst of towns, and there they received the sacrificial food which their worshipers also ate. Their ceremonies symbolized the seasons and ensured good harvest and enough food for men and beasts.

The gods shared the prosperity and disasters of their people, went into battle with them against hostile states, even suffered the destruction of their temples by foreign invaders. In Mesopotamian mythology the gods had subdued primeval chaos, a dark and formless waste of waters, and had introduced order and rule into the universe. Since they accepted authority and order from the Assembly of the Gods, the citizens of the theocratic state were expected to be law-abiding, obedient to their rulers, and honest. Rewards and punishments, which were given by the gods as the ultimate rulers, were strictly confined to this world, for the Sumerians, unlike the Egyptians, had no clear-cut ideas about an afterlife. The spirits of men lived on, but it was a wretched existence in a shadow world. One Sumerian text says of the dead: "Earth is their food, their nourishment clay. Ghosts flutter their wings like birds there, and on the gates and the gateposts the dust lies undisturbed."

Statues in Sumer were of two kinds, and both served religious purposes. First, there were the statues of the gods, which were set up to be worshiped in the temple sanctuaries. These had to conform with tradition, and each deity was identified by his or her attributes, which might be a sacred animal supporting the throne or base of the image. These gods were human in shape, but their poses often suggested nothing but serene omnipotence. The second kind of statue gave the sculptor much greater opportunity for originality, as these were individual portraits of men and women. The reason for their presence in the temple sanctuaries is intriguing.

For the Sumerians there could be no prosperity for the city or for the individual without the favor of the gods, and the gods were exacting, requiring faithful attendance and prayer at their temples. The Sumerians were an extremely businesslike people; many were traders, craftsmen, and men of affairs. Constant devotion was impossible for busy officials, so they would worship the gods by proxy. Just as the deity was represented by an image made by man, so his worshiper would be represented by a statue, a sculptured substitute for the man himself. A well-to-do Sumerian would commission his statue, a portrait of himself in an attitude of humble prayer, and have it set in the temple in the presence of the god's statue. The effect would be the same as if the worshiper were there in person. One statue from Lagash is inscribed, "It offers prayers," and on another the prayer begins, "Statue, say to my king [god] . . . ." This meant that Sumerian sculptors were strictly limited in range, because only one or two conventional poses were allowed. However the portrait heads, the most important part of the statues, gave them scope for variety.

The lack of stone in Sumer had a decided effect on its sculpture. The Sumerians could get rough limestone from the high desert bordering the river valley some distance away, but for their best work they were obliged to import. Basalt and semiprecious stones came from Iran. Diorite, which would take a fine polish, was brought by sea from Oman. It was apparently not quarried but came in boulders, and their size and shape influenced the sculptor's work. The stone was expensive and had to be used to the best advantage; a block would seldom be long enough to make a life-sized, standing figure. The Sumerians were not very successful with their seated figures because they would often suggest the shape of the boulders from which they were carved. In most statues the sculptor concentrated on the head, since this was the most important part from his own and his client's point of view. The rest of the figure was often disproportionately small. The Sumerian rule seems to have been to make the body only four times the size of the head. The true proportion of the body is, in fact, nearer to six or seven times the head size.

The statue of Lugal-Dalu (Plate III-6), king of Adab, dates from very early in the third millennium B.C. His name is inscribed in pictographic writing on his right shoulder. We see before us a typical Sumerian—broad, short, stocky, and optimistic. He is standing in the prescribed pose, facing the god with his hands clasped in supplication, and dressed only in a long-tiered skirt. The artist has not perfected his grasp of anatomy. The figure's elbows are too pointed, and the flesh of the arms does not seem to contain a bone at all. His head rests on solidly constructed, broad shoulders, however. It is hard to dislike Lugal-Dalu, whose pleasant visage stares at us across so many centuries. With his huge eyes and

III-6. Statue of Lugal-Dalu, king of Adab. Early third millennium B.C.

stubbed features, he seems to be close kin to the worshiper from Lagash (Plate III-7) and to Kurlil (Plate III-8), the administrator of the granaries of Uruk, who lived two hundred years later. Both these individuals are portrayed seated, with legs crossed, and both are definitely Sumerians—low of brow, broad of face, and resembling in no way the slim, impassive, and self-assured pharaohs and officials of Egypt. In fact, it would not take a great stretch of the imagination to say that the gentleman from Lagash appears unctuous, while Kurlil, for whatever reason, seems worried. The statuette of a female supplicant, possibly a

III-7. Statue of a worshiper, from Lagash. Early third millennium B.C.

III-8. Stone statue of Kurlil, administrator of the granaries of Uruk, found near Ur. *c.* 2600 B.C.

III-9. Statuette of a female worshiper, perhaps a royal princess, from Lagash. *c.* 2600 B.C.

III-10. Woman worshiper, from Tel Asmar in Diyala. *c.* 2900 B.C.

princess, from Lagash shows us another physical type (Plate III-9). This figure is an extreme example of the tendency of Mesopotamian sculptors to portray a large head with an excessively short body. The woman worshiper from Tel Asmar in Diyala (Plate III-10) has the tiny hands, thick ankles, and huge eyes common to statues from that area. Records show that the Sumerians were excellent businessmen, and we cannot doubt it. But we might wonder whether they could have been artists and poets.

In the statue of Iku-Shamagan (Plate III-11) we see another physical type altogether. He wears the same tiered skirt as Lugal-Dalu, but he is thinner, his face is leaner, his features narrower, and he is bearded. In a word, he is a typical Akka-

III-11. **Statue of Iku-Shamagan, king of Mari. Third millennium** B.C.

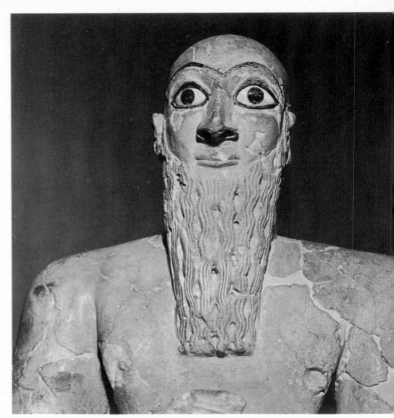

III-12. **Detail of the statue of Iku-Shamagan, king of Mari. Third millennium** B.C.

dian. This splendid figure was found in the temple of Ishtar, patron goddess of the city of Mari, of which Iku-Shamagan was king. In the ruins of Mari dozens of statues have been found of men and women, all likenesses of the Semitic Akkadians. Although the proportions of these statues appear massive, they vary in height from a mere 8 inches to 3 feet. With their fixed expressions and powerful staring eyes (Plate III-12), often made of bitumen inlaid with shell, they look very much alike, but on close inspection they are very different.

King Iku-Shamagan and King Lamgi-Mari (Plate III-13) have no resemblance to each other, and neither belongs to a standardized kingly type we shall see in later Mesopotamian sculpture. The administrator of the grain supply, Idi-Narum (Plate III-14), cannot possibly be confused with the smiling, obsequious steward Ebihil

III-13. Statue of Lamgi-Mari, king of Mari. *c.* 2500 B.C.

III-15. Statue of the steward Ebihil, from Mari. *c.* 2300 B.C.

III-14. Portrait bust of Idi-Narum, administrator of the grain supply of Mari. Third millennium B.C.

(Plate III-15). The statues of women, too, have quite distinct personalities. The queens and royal women wearing the high "polos" headdresses seen only in Mari are dignified and faintly smiling (Plates III-16 and III-17). The seated woman in Plate III-18 wears an impressive shawl covering her headdress as well as her body. Ur-Nanshe, the great singer who was probably a dancer as well (Plate III-19), sits bareheaded with the disciplined grace and authority of a ballerina.

III-16. Head of a woman, probably a princess of Mari. Third millennium B.C.

III-17. Head of a queen, from Mari. Third millennium B.C.

III-19. Statue of Ur-Nanshe, the great singer, from Mari. Third millennium B.C.

III-18. Statue of a seated woman of the royal family. Third millennium B.C.

Most touching, perhaps, is the group of husband and wife from the temple of Ishtar at Mari (Plate III-20). The figures are uncomfortably seated and are anatomically far from perfect. The wife's left arm has been squeezed in and reduced to tiny size. But their soft flesh is sensitively modeled, and there is even more of a sense of overwhelming tenderness than we saw in the figures of husbands and wives of ancient Egypt.

Copper and bronze were also used for reliefs and statues in the round when these materials came into general use. The standing worshiper in Plate III-21 is made of bronze, and here we see how much more freely a sculptor could compose his figure in metal than he could in stone. Arms are separated from the body rather than clasped to it. The figure does not need the support

III-20. Group of husband and wife, from Mari. Third millennium B.C.

III-21. **Bronze statuette of a worshiper. Mesopotamia. Third millennium** B.C.

138

III-22. **Clay figurine Mesopotamia.** *c.* 3500 B.C. British Museum, London.

III-23. **Clay figurine of a goddess with snake's head. Mesopotamia.** *c.* 3500 B.C.

of the solid block of a heavy-tiered skirt.

There is a striking contrast between this more or less official sculpture, which respects the human form and keeps to certain rules, and the strange, often grotesque images found in Mesopotamian graves for thousands of years, from before the age of Sumer until the age of Babylon (Plate III-22). These figures are unlike anything human or animal. They are hybrids, like the goddess in Plate III-23, a crudely made figurine with a head like a snake's and a bitumen wig, found in a grave of the fourth millennium B.C. There are many bird-faced

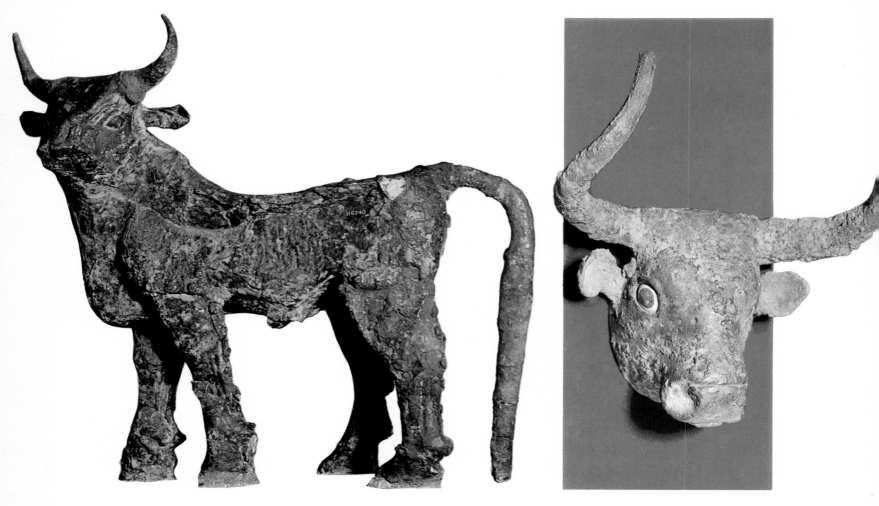

III-24. Copper bull, from Tell el Obeid. Third millennium B.C.

III-25. Copper head of a bull, from Lagash. c. 2900 B.C.

figures and other fantastic idols, and none has a purely human appearance. Again and again in the long history of Mesopotamian art we shall see the same extravagant fancy, a real world interwoven with a fantasy world, where mythical powers, like those of Egypt, take half-human, half-animal forms.

Not all the works of art found in the rubble of the great temples consisted of figures of gods and their supplicants. There were decorative pieces as well. The copper bull from Tell el Obeid (Plate III-24) formed part of a procession of animals adorning the temple's facade. The copper was applied on a mold of wood and pitch, and the figure has the splendidly free decorative line the Mesopotamians always gave to the animals they depicted, and especially to the bull. The copper head of a bull from Lagash (Plate III-25) also formed part of the decoration of a temple. Here the eyes are of mother-of-pearl and lapis lazuli. In Plate III-26 we see a plaster cast of a frieze of white limestone and shell set in bitumen, again from Tell el Obeid. It depicts a homely scene of cows from the temple herd being milked. It might remind us of similar relief friezes from ancient Egypt, with figures shown partly in profile and partly in full face, were it not that even at a distance we can identify the squat, broad figures of Sumerian art.

III-26. **Plaster cast of an inlaid frieze from Tell el Obeid. Third millennium B.C.**

What of the temples themselves? These temples, the greatest monuments of Sumerian art, were built of dried mud-brick on stone foundations, as we have seen. It was the Sumerian practice to fill in these temples periodically with brickwork, covering over the statues and votive amulets. The buried temple then became the foundation for the new temple. Some of these great mounds, or *ziggurats,* have survived, and we find them scattered over the Mesopotamian plain today. But where staged towers once rose above the walled temple enclosures at Ur, Kish, Eridu, Uruk, Larsa, and Nippur, the proud walls and noble staircases of sun-dried brick have perished, and only the core of the mounds on which they were built remains. Now peculiarly unnatural heaps on the face of the surrounding plain, they are no more than sad reminders of the powerful, durable communities that once lived there and undertook to build them.

The names given to the ziggurats explain their significance. At Nippur, for instance, the ziggurat was called "House of the Mountain, bond between Heaven and Earth." The Mountain is the place where the mysterious powers of earth and nature are concentrated. The mother goddess Ninhursag is the Lady of the Mountain; Tammuz, the god of vegetation, who dies in the summer drought, is kept captive in the Mountain until the New Year begins. The ziggurats were a means of communication with the gods. They were huge staircases by which the unseen protectors of cities might descend to earth. A temple of welcome stood at the summit, and there was another shrine at ground level, which was the god's dwelling on earth. The two were connected by staircases, sometimes triple ones, for processions of priests and worshipers. The towers, from three to

seven stories high, were built of two types of brick: unbaked, sun-dried mud-bricks for the inside, kiln-fired bricks for the outer surface, often marked with the royal seal. No brick was more than 15 inches long, and the builders' task was formidable. Masons, engineers, and architects had to cope with endless problems, and we can see how well they succeeded. Because these structures were made of brick rather than stone, they needed all the support possible, and there was little room for windows or doors. Such dark interiors, with heavy walls and few windows, also provided the best protection against the insistent heat of the sun. Columns for supporting a ceiling were, of course, impossible, although they were used for porticoes. The ruins of Sumerian cities are still dominated by these great mounds, eroded as they are, after more than 4,000 years. The ziggurat of Tchoga Zanbil (Plate III-27) is very late, dating

III-27. The ziggurat of Tchoga Zanbil, near Susa. *c.* 1200 B.C.

from the thirteenth century B.C., but a picture of it can give us some faint idea of the impression of the squared-off design of a ziggurat.

Not all Sumerian art was directly related to religion. Some of the best relief carving of this early period is to be found, surprisingly enough, on tiny cylinder seals. These were rolled across the soft clay of tablets, stoppers, and labels to impress miniature pictures. Seals were necessary in all business transactions. Purchases had to be confirmed by written agreement, duly witnessed, registered, and sealed. Seals were also used for protection, as when a stamped lump of clay was placed over the fastening of a box or bale as proof that it had not been opened or tampered with. Even the doors of houses were sealed.

The meaning of the intricate scenes is not always clear. Filled with half-human monsters, they often show the extravagant fancy we have spoken of. A common motif is the fight between a lion and a bull-man, perhaps the mythical protector of flocks and herds. In Plate III-28 we see a seal as it actually looked, and above it three impressions made by rolling such a seal across a clay surface. The top impression shows two men about to kill two rampant bulls. A little ibex stands on either side of the heraldic-looking group. The second is a procession of bulls, possibly belonging to the temple, with ears of barley filling in the spaces. It is interesting to notice that the bulls are single-horned because only one horn would be seen from the side, although this single horn is depicted as if seen frontally. The bottom imprint shows men, women, and animals in scenes from mythology or taking part in cult rituals. The miniature scenes are carved with a sense of spacing, proportion, and design. The delicate craftsmanship of these seals is extraor-

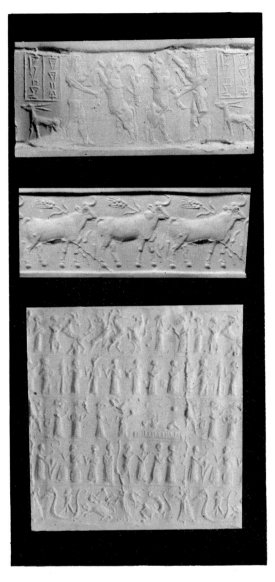

III-28. Sumerian seal and three imprints. *c.* 2800–2300 B.C.

dinary when we consider that the carvings were made on a tiny curved surface.

There are early works of sculpture, and particularly relief, that serve a monumental function, commemorating military conquests, the completion of a new building, or the opening of a canal. These take the form of stone pillars, or *stelae,* sculpted in relief, or carved stone plaques. Sumerian sculptors had a freer hand in such relief sculpture than they had with statues in the round, for the stelae were monuments in-

tended to impress and to be seen by the public. They were exciting dramas in stone.

The Stele of the Vultures (Plate III-29) commemorates the victory won by King Eannatum of Lagash over the neighboring town of Umma. It is a boundary stone set up after the battle as a record of the agreement between victor and vanquished, and it gives a summary of the battle in four horizontal sections. Unfortunately, only fragments remain, but they are enough to

III-29. Stele of the Vultures, from Lagash. Third millennium B.C.

give us an amazingly vivid impression of Sumerian warfare. One side of the stele shows the exploits of warriors led by their king; the other side shows the decisive intervention of the gods on Eannatum's side. In the top section the men of Lagash advance in a phalanx; the king stands in front in his helmet and thick sheepskin hide. The soldiers march over their enemies' bodies, which vultures are already devouring. The army is represented in an almost "impressionistic" way in that the eye immediately grasps the "impression" of a large number of soldiers because the artist has crowded as many heads, feet, and hands holding lances as he can into a block form that suggests an impenetrable military formation. In the lower section Eannatum rides in his war chariot followed by his light infantry. Here each soldier is more completely defined. Again we see the short, solid figures of Mesopotamian art with their large noses and bulging eyes. Compared to Egyptian relief of the same period the figures are crudely done and flat rather than sculpturally rounded.

But it would be unfair to generalize in this way about Sumerian art. The stone bull from Uruk, dating from about 3000 B.C., is perhaps finer than anything of the time found in Egypt (Plate III-30). Its horns and legs are missing, but the muscular anatomy of the body is perfect, and it suggests the immense power and bulk of the beast with genius.

Apart from religious items, seals, and historical documents like the Stele of the Vultures, Sumerian civilization produced a great range of decorative objects that are superb works of art. The richest source of these decorative works is the Royal Cemetery at Ur, in which was found what is probably the most chilling burial in history.

In 1927 Sir Leonard Woolley discovered

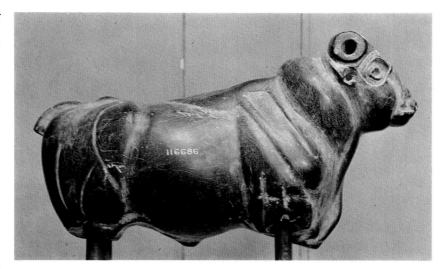

III-30. **Stone Bull, from Uruk.** *c.* 3000 B.C.

a series of burials at Ur, sometimes called Ur of the Chaldees ("Chaldean" being the biblical term for Mesopotamian civilization), dating from nearly 2800 B.C. Men and women in splendid ceremonial dress, either kings and queens or priests and priestesses, were found buried in stone- or brick-lined chambers sunk at the bottom of deep pits. They were accompanied by a wealth of precious and extremely beautiful objects, a fact not exceptional in itself. What was exceptional was the presence of other bodies. Was this the mass burial of the victims of some disaster? In one pit two sleighs were found, with the skeletons of the oxen that drew them, the grooms that tended them, and the riders that drove them. In another pit were found helmeted soldiers. In yet another, most alarming of all, were found the bodies of no less than sixty-eight women, some wearing gold diadems, some carrying musical instruments, and all dressed in robes of brilliant red wool. This could have been no accident, no pantomime enacted with the corpses of those who happened to die at the same time. We can only assume, from the positions of the bodies and the way they were dressed, that they walked into these huge grave pits *alive.*

More of this strange ritual we cannot tell. The oxen hauled the carts down the ramp, and then all were slain, oxen and drivers alike. Near the bodies of the women were found cups. Did they march in solemn procession, carrying musical instruments and singing, then lie down and take poison? There is no sign of violence. Were these the attendants of priests and priestesses sacrificed in some annual fertility festival? Were they the attendants of a king and queen, following their masters like the *shawabty*-figures of Egypt? Did the Sumerians bury human beings to attend to the needs of others in the afterlife? No inscription tells us what purpose these devoted souls served in the next world, but the superb objects found with them tell us much of what their life was like in this.

Gold and silver were found in abundance—ornaments, vessels, and weapons—and the jewelers' and goldsmiths' work was very fine. The attendants went to their deaths wearing delicate wreaths of willow or beech leaves wrought in gold, with crests of metal flowers. Some of the most beautiful treasures are simply fluted vases and bowls, and ceremonial gold daggers with hilts of silver and lapis lazuli; this and carnelian seem to have been the favorite stones for Sumerian ornament. In pure craftsmanship, in turning sheet metal into bowls and vases, in chasing and inlay, the Sumerian goldsmith had nothing to learn from his modern descendant.

In this treasure were found two superb figures of rams eating from the Tree of Life,

which have fascinated lovers of art since they first came to light. One, now in the British Museum, we see in Plate III-31. These were made of carved wood overlaid with gold, silver, shell, and lapis lazuli, all glued on with bitumen. The charm of these small figures, which may have been supports of an offering table, is as fresh as it must have been when they were first made nearly five thousand years ago, at the very time of the great pyramids of Egypt. A small, wide-eyed animal gazes at us, standing uncomfortably as it reaches for the golden leaves and flowers. As we can see, the Sumerian sculptor, obliged to obey the most rigid conventions when portraying human worshipers, could let his imagination and skill run free when he reproduced subjects from the animal world.

Musicians with their harps, lyres, and cymbals attended the king or priest in the ritual burial. Wooden harps, beautifully decorated with animal figureheads in gold, and panels inlaid with grotesque animal figures, like a donkey playing a harp, have been found and reconstructed.

Among the treasures recovered from the tombs at Ur, perhaps the most interesting from a historical point of view is the so-called Standard, an oblong box 1½ feet long with four panels and ends tapering toward the top, in which small figures in shell or mother-of-pearl are inlaid against a mosaic of lapis lazuli. Borders of the same materials surround a series of events shown in horizontal sequence. It has been suggested that this box was not a standard measure at all, but the sound-box of a musical instrument, since its shape is like the sound-boxes of lyres from other tombs. But whatever its purpose, the scenes on the main panels represent the drama of war and peace in ancient Ur. They commemorate a battle in which the soldiers of Ur, led by the king,

III-31. Ram of gold and lapis lazuli in a thicket, from Ur. *c.* 2800 B.C.

III-33. Panel from the Standard of Ur, illustrating a victory celebration.  *c.* 2800 B.C.

III-32. Side of the Standard of Ur, illustrating Sumerian warfare.  *c.* 2800 B.C.

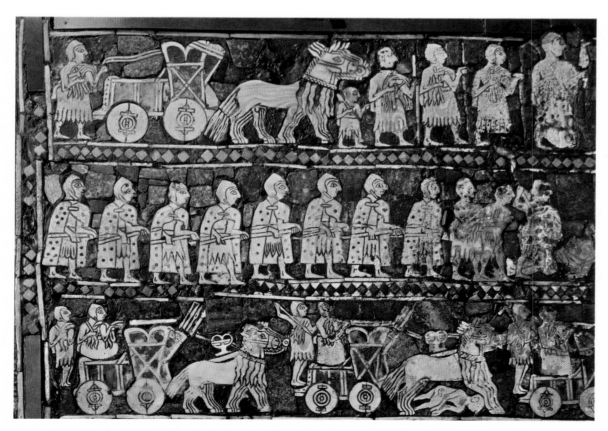

were victorious, and the victory celebrations that followed. As a witness to the dress and life habits of the Sumerians, the Standard is invaluable.

Plate III-32 is war. In the top sequence, the king, always larger than the other figures, stands in front, followed by three attendants. Four asses draw the royal chariot. In the center, the phalanx advances, as light infantry attack the enemy. The bottom sequence is the earliest known scene of a chariot fight. (The chariot was not to be introduced into Egypt for another thousand years.) We see teams of wild asses advancing first at a walk, then speeding up to a gallop as they ride down the defeated enemy. The construction of the chariots, the armor, pointed helmets, and weapons of the soldiers are all depicted in detail. A rein ring, exactly like those we see on the backs of the asses drawing the chariots, was found in one of the chariots buried in the tombs.

The panel in Plate III-33 shows peace in Ur. In the top register we see the king and his court feasting, while beneath we see attendants bringing captured booty, and food supplies mostly on the hoof—cattle, goats, and sheep. One servant is even carrying fish. The king and his companions

III-34. Stele of Sargon of Agade. Twenty-fourth century B.C.

are reclining and drinking in leisurely fashion, listening to a musician with a lyre who sings, perhaps, of victory.

If the peasants of Mesopotamia lived in mud-brick huts in the company of goats, the ruler and his court wore robes of fine cloth, drank beer, and lived in a world of songbirds and flowers, where jeweled rams fed on thickets of gold. What sinister price was paid for this luxury in the grave pits of Ur history does not disclose.

This early period in Mesopotamia is called the *Dynastic* period because there were many dynasties in the various cities, one following another, while no single king of one city was able to gain supremacy. It came to an end in the twenty-fourth century

B.C. when Sharrum-kin, known as Sargon of Agade, conquered the entire area and united it for the first time in history.

Sargon, a great soldier, was a man of obscure Akkadian origin who suddenly emerged as the founder of a dynasty and an empire. A cup-bearer or administrator under the king of Kish, he had, according to legend, overthrown Lugalzagesi who had subjugated Kish, and proclaimed himself king. He set up his new capital at Agade, a city still undiscovered, and embarked on a career of conquest which made him ruler of the greatest empire yet known in Mesopotamia. Sargon defeated the Sumerian cities through superior fighting ability, and conquered the whole country as far south as the Persian Gulf, where his soldiers "washed their weapons." But unlike Egypt, the area of the Tigris and Euphrates rivers had no natural boundaries. In an effort to subdue dangerous neighbors, Sargon extended his empire in all directions, conquering Elam with its capital Susa in the east, and the lands along the upper Euphrates as far north as the Mediterranean itself, so that he could claim to rule "from the lower sea (the Persian Gulf) to the upper sea (the Mediterranean)." There is some literary evidence that he may have controlled an even greater empire, including Asia Minor.

Sargon was an Akkadian, but the Akkadians continued to share Sumerian customs and religious practices. He followed the ancient custom of Ur in making his daughter high priestess of the moon-god Nanna, the patron deity of Ur; we know this from an inscribed relief in alabaster from the Temple of Ningal. Sargon's successors followed his example in the honors they paid to Sumerian gods. The kings of Agade were accepted as legitimate rulers, and there was no racial antagonism between the Semitic Akkadians and the Sumerians, although the reign of the Dynasty of Agade inevitably brought some changes. Akkadian names appear more often in the official records, and the Semitic language known as Akkadian became the literary language, although the older Sumerian language continued in use at first.

In commemorating his victories, too, Sargon followed Sumerian tradition. The diorite stele from the Louvre (Plate III-34) shows battle scenes carved in the Sumerian manner. Episodes are set out in rows, as in the time of Eannatum; vultures and a net for trapping the enemy appear. In the detail we see here, an Akkadian soldier, his weapon raised threateningly, is pushing forward two prisoners whose hands are tied.

This relief has the crude carving, but also the strength and vigor, of earlier Sumerian works. The Agade or Sargonic era in art was a time of restless development. The effect of the new Akkadian influence on Mesopotamian art can be seen most clearly in the great Stele of Naram-Sin, Sargon's grandson.

The stele (Plate III-35), which is 6 feet high, is a monolithic boulder of pink sandstone, the natural shape of which has been only slightly altered by the sculptor's chisel. It commemorates Naram-Sin's victory in about 2300 B.C. over the Lullubi, a tribe of Iranian mountaineers. On it we see soldiers, armed with spears, bows, arrows, and axes, following their king. The men are all on foot, as they would naturally march in a hilly country, and there is something of a landscape. Following their king, who is under the protection of divine symbols, the soldiers are scaling a high, wooded mountain. A swift comparison of this scene with the Stele of the Vultures (Plate III-29) will tell us much about the way Mesopotamian art progressed. The forms do not present an almost flat surface, but stand out in gentle, rounded relief. They are no longer the squat and stilted figures of earlier Sumerian relief, but are taller and more slender. Moreover, this relief has great freedom of movement, in striking contrast with the ordered formality of the earlier work. The figures do not form a stylized block, but rather each soldier is depicted separately, making his way up a mountainside planted with trees. The poses are not identical. Each man is moving on his own, an individual rather than a symbolic part of a mass. This greater naturalism is particularly clear in the detail in Plate III-36, showing soldiers climbing upward, while their enemies are hurtled down from above.

III-36. Detail of the Stele of Naram-Sin, king of Agade. *c.* 2300 B.C.

III-35. Stele of Naram-Sin, king of Agade. *c.* 2300 B.C.

The alert, energetic figures of Naram-Sin's army are contrasted with the limp, twisted, and lifeless bodies of the foe. Nothing so subtle could have been expressed earlier in Sumerian art.

The rule of Sargon's descendants lasted no more than a few generations. Then the Dynasty of Agade was brought to an end by several factors, culminating in an invasion by the Gutians, a barbaric race from western Iran, and a time of anarchy followed. The Sumerian scribes wrote "Who was king? Who was not king?" in their dynastic lists, and the temple hymns bewail the desecration of shrines.

But the cities of Sumer probably kept their independence and gradually assimilated the Gutians. Lagash flourished, and during the period called the Neo-Sumerian (*c.* 2230–2000 B.C.), there was a revival of art, especially after the expulsion of the Gutian rulers around 2110 B.C. In this cultural revival, the leading cities were Lagash and Ur, whose kings ruled from 2113 to 2006 B.C. over the whole of Mesopotamia.

In art the city of Lagash dominates the years around 2150 B.C. with a remarkable series of statues. These were commissioned by one man of enigmatic but fascinating character, Gudea. This remarkable man claims in his inscriptions to have built temples and won victories which ensured the safety and peace of Lagash, yet he never took the title of king, contenting himself with the position of *ensi,* an official exercising religious and political functions. Nevertheless his power and authority were equal to, if not greater than, those of other Sumerian kings.

Gudea made Lagash an unrivaled center of the arts. Palaces, temples, and public buildings were adorned with sculpture, par-ticularly with statues of Gudea himself. Over thirty of these, first discovered by French archeologists in this century, are known to exist. They are among the most impressive collections of sculpture ever created on the orders of one man in one place, and they are the finest work of the Neo-Sumerian period.

The statues are carved of diorite and dolerite, stones so hard they challenge the skill of the most experienced sculptors. Many of the statues are headless, but the heads of several have been retrieved. The head and body of the seated statuette in Plate III-37 were found during two separate expeditions five years apart. The artists have taken account of Gudea's age, and so the portraits show what he looked like from about twenty-five to forty. He is generally portrayed wearing a simple, straight robe wrapped over one shoulder and unadorned except for a border and fringe, and he often wears a characteristic turban (Plates III-38, III-39, and III-40).

These figures, with their large heads, short necks, and small bodies, seem at first sight to resemble earlier Sumerian work. But if we look more closely and compare these with the earlier figures of Sumerian worshipers, we will see that a great change has taken place. Despite their strange proportions, these figures appear to be made of flesh beneath which we sense muscle and bone. Beneath the cheeks we can see that there are cheek bones and jawbones. The arms and shoulders are handsome and muscular. The surface modeling is smoother and finer, and the figures present altogether a more natural appearance. In the figure of a woman wearing a kerchief and necklace (Plate III-41), we can make out the form of the model's body beneath the delicate cloth of her robe, which now seems to fall in a more naturalistic manner. The peculiar, tiered effect of earlier Sumerian dress has disappeared.

The inscriptions on the statues tell us what Gudea's achievements were. He was a wise administrator who kept his ambitions within bounds, and he was devoted to the cause of peace. He sought to be remembered as a man of religion. His strong features may be idealized by the sculptor, but his face is unmistakable in all the statues. It is the face of a practical man of affairs, a self-confident ruler who drew his strength from his religion and his reverence for the gods.

III-37. **Portrait of Gudea of Lagash, seated.** *c.* 2200 B.C.

III-38. **Statue, probably of Gudea of Lagash.** *c.* 2200 B.C.

III-39. Turbaned head of Gudea of Lagash.
*c.* 2200 B.C.

III-41. Statue of a woman wearing a kerchief
and necklace, from Lagash.  *c.* 2200 B.C.

III-40. Standing statue of Gudea of Lagash.
*c.* 2200 B.C.

The reign of Gudea's son, Ur-Ningirsu, produced at least one masterpiece, the headless statue of the king himself (Plate III-42). Its base is decorated with a procession of figures bringing tribute, carrying baskets containing vases which they offer on their knees. There are also several interesting portrait heads like the one in Plate III-43, which is probably of Ur-Ningirsu himself. There is a slight resemblance between this young man's features and those of his father, but the face is less strong and determined. The serenity is there but not the force of character.

At the turn of the second millennium B.C., the Sumerian revival came to an end. Again wandering tribesmen attacked the centers of Sumerian civilization, and this time Ur was destroyed. A poet wrote:

> In its lofty gates, where they were
>    wont to promenade, dead bodies
>    lay about.
> In its spacious streets, where feasts
>    were celebrated, scattered they
>    lay . . . ,
> Its corpses, like fat placed in the sun,
>    melted away . . . ,
> The old men and women who could
>    not leave their homes were over-
>    come by fire.
> The babes lying on their mother's laps
>    like fish were carried off by the
>    waters . . .
> The judgment of the land perished.
>    The people mourn . . .[7]

In Egypt, the Middle Kingdom was beginning. It was at this point that Babylon entered history.

At the time that, according to biblical tradition, the tribe of Abraham left Ur to

III-42. Statue of Ur-Ningirsu of Lagash. Twenty-second century B.C.

---

[7] S. N. Kramer (translator), *Sumerian Mythology*, American Philosophical Society, Philadelphia, 1944

III-43. **Diorite head of a young man, probably Ur-Ningursu of Lagash. Twenty-second century** B.C.

find new lands to the north, the tribe of Terah also left the city and made itself the ruling power of a small village on the Euphrates called Babylon. With this new dynasty the town rose to some local eminence. It was under her great king Hammurabi (1792–1750 B.C.) that Babylon became an empire.

By supplanting local kings with governors answering directly to himself, Hammurabi welded a confederacy of neighboring cities into a nation, and with the aid of a well-trained national infantry he conquered an empire that stretched, like Sargon's, from the Persian Gulf to the Zagros mountains. It is not as a conqueror, however, but as a law giver that Hammurabi is best known. He planted in every town in his empire an inscription setting

out the law of the land. He did not invent this law, but he *codified* it, which is to say he drew it together, set it down, and established the same law for every city and village. In Plate III-44 we see a relief of King Hammurabi standing before the Sun-god of justice, who holds a measuring stick and rod. This may not seem at first an extraordinary work of art, but look at the Plate again, for you see pictured here one of the great documents of history. On this black basalt stele is the code itself. It tells us of a man's responsibility to his wife and children, and for his wife's debts, and fixes the rules for a tolerant divorce. It controls the sale of alcoholic beverages and the percentage of interest on loans. It dictates the liability of a builder for a house that falls down, and of a doctor for a patient that he may injure. Above all, it states that no man will take the law into his own hands, and that the state will see that justice is done. It is one of man's greatest steps toward a state of true civilization.

In matters of art and culture generally, the Babylonians adopted the heritage of the Sumerians, who had disappeared at last from the political scene. The Sumerian language was still used by scribes for religious and magical literature, and it was learned and copied in schools. Nearly all existing copies of Sumerian writings date from this period, although the texts must have been composed long before, when the language was still alive. Meanwhile the Semitic Akkadian, the spoken language of Babylon, developed a literature in which great epics and hymns were composed, among them the famous Epic of Creation. Above all, the Babylonians, not the Egyptians, were the founders of modern astronomy and mathematics. It was the Babylonians who invented a system by which they could work easily with fractions. Meanwhile, life in the old Sumerian cities seems to have been resumed and continued peacefully enough; at Ur a great new canal was dug and named "Hammurabi is the abundance of the people."

The code of Hammurabi was found at the Elamite city of Susa, and in fact Babylonian art is known to us largely from discoveries at Susa and Mari. Many of these date from the period just before Hammurabi, but they are generally considered of the Babylonian period. In Babylon itself excavation has brought to light no objects of major artistic importance other than cylinder seals and small terra-cotta figurines.

III-44. The Code of Hammurabi, found at Susa. Eighteenth century B.C.

III-45. Statue of Ishtup-Ilum, governor of Mari. *c.* 1900 B.C.(?)

III-46. A man in a tasseled cloak, found at Mari.
*c.* 1900 B.C.(?)

III-47. Goddess with a flowing vase, from Mari.
*c.* 1800 B.C.

The city of Mari with its great palace has been thoroughly excavated, and a wealth of sculpture and painting has been revealed. The statues found suggest that no definite break with tradition took place, but rather a steady evolution right up to the time of Hammurabi. The austere Sumerian tradition persisted, as we can see in the statue of Ishtup-Ilum, governor of Mari (Plate III-45). The inscription on his shoulder gives his name and says "God kept him alive." But here we do see something new, an elaborately curled and stylized beard. The portrait of a man in a tasseled cloak carrying a sheep or goat as an offering to the temple is also of the old Sumerian type (Plate III-46). But the gracious figure of a goddess holding a vase (Plate III-47) is taller, more slender, and freer of movement than figures that went before. Her arms are shown as held free of her body, and the anatomy of the figure seems well understood. She is also wearing a new type of more fitted garment. The horned helmet she wears is a symbol of divinity (we see it on the god of justice as well), and the vase she carries was connected with a tank of water. On certain occasions it overflowed with "the water of fertility." The richly robed statue of Idi-Ilum, prince of Mari (Plate III-48), shows a new elegance and richness of dress.

In earlier Sumer, painting had been restricted largely to abstract designs and patterns that enhanced the background of reliefs. But the palace at Mari was lavishly decorated with wall paintings of this period, and these have been miraculously preserved. The royal family's apartments are adorned with geometric patterns, originally in bril-

III-48. Statue of Idi-Ilum, prince of Mari. *c.* 1900 B.C.(?)

III-49. Detail of mural painting, from the palace of Mari. *c.* 1800 B.C.

liant colors, but the administrative sector of the palace has painted scenes of warfare and religious ceremonies, with glimpses of trees, plants, and birds. As in the case of sculpture, we find in the frescoes the sacred art of the Sumerians enlivened by a new, natural vivacity. The details of these paintings we see in Plates III-49 and III-50 are part of a procession scene showing worshipers leading sacrificial bulls. In many ways, the hard outlines, the stylized distortion of the figures with heads and legs in profile and shoulders and eyes seen from front view, remind us of Egyptian wall painting. But, as ever, it is the character of the figures, the actual facial types of Mesopotamia, that differ. These bearded figures, with their blunt, distinctive features, do not resemble the Egyptians in any way. The huge figure on the right is the king, but only his arm

and the flounce of his robe have survived.

A closer contact with nature in rendering animals and scenes from everyday life appears in early Babylonian art. The bronze lions, one of which is illustrated in Plate III-51, which guarded the entrance to the Temple of Dagan at Mari, are savagely vigilant, their sinews tensed for action as though ready to pounce on any intruder. To complete the terrifying effect, the bronze-founder fitted their jaws with rows of fangs carved in bone (now missing) and gave them glaring eyes made of white stone inlaid with blue schist. The three bronze ibexes from Larsa (Plate III-52) give the same lively effect.

The terra-cotta plaques and molds recovered from various towns in the old Babylonian era also express a new, spontaneous realism, as if the artists were rediscovering

III-50. **Detail of mural painting, from the palace of Mari.** *c.* 1800 B.C.

III-51. **Bronze head of a lion, from Mari.** *c.* 1950 B.C.

III-52. **Bronze group of three ibexes, from Larsa.** 1900–1800 B.C.

the life going on around them and reproducing what they saw for their own pleasure. A lion attacks an ox, an all too common incident in the farmer's life; a peasant rides a hump-backed ox, goading it with his heels and stick; a wandering showman exhibits tame monkeys; a carpenter shapes a piece of wood. These moments in ordinary people's lives, seized and translated into clay, are absent from Sumerian works of art, which only show ordinary people on great occasions, as in the Standard of Ur (Plates III-32 and III-33). The mold in Plate III-53 displays a hunter leading a captured stag while a greyhound leaps up in excitement. We get some idea of the refinement of life at Mari when we realize that this mold was used for stamping royal cakes and pastries!

After Hammurabi's death in 1750 B.C. his dynasty declined, and the next 150 years were sterile in works of art. Babylonia, rich, fertile, and civilized, was again men-what they found, and remarkably adaptable. They kept a precarious hold on Babylonia for 600 years. The Elamites from the Iranian plateau made swift, successful raids from time to time, and carried off the Stelae of Naram-Sin (Plate III-35) and Hammurabi to Susa as war trophies.

The Cassites were essentially imitators and adapters, not creators in the arts. They restored ruined monuments in the ancient cities of Ur, Uruk, and Nippur, and adorned the shrines of their gods. They built a magnificent ziggurat approached by a triple stairway at their capital, Dur-kurigalzu, near Baghdad, and a great palace decorated with frescoes. Characteristic of Cassite culture are the boundary stones, or *kudurrus,* which were placed in sanctuaries, covered with inscriptions and carved in relief with figures of kings and gods in presentation scenes or with divine symbols and attributes. In Plate III-54 we see three such kudurrus, dating from about 1150 B.C., quite late in the period of Cassite art. These particular stones were records of grants of land by the king. Inscriptions on one side confirm the gift, while the other side shows images or symbols of the gods (imaginatively carved in a stylized manner) who will protect the giver and recipient. The workmanship in these three stones differs in quality. But it is interesting that in stone *B,* although the figures are curiously portrayed, their shoulders, as well as their heads and feet, are shown in profile.

While a Cassite dynasty reigned in Babylon, an Elamite dynasty continued to reign at Susa. Their stone reliefs and panels of molded bricks, like the one shown in Plate III-55, are often vigorous. This ingenious technique of fitting molded bricks together to form a bas-relief solved the problem of creating large-scale sculptural decoration in a land where there was plentiful material

III-53. Terra-cotta mold, from Mari.
*c.* 1800 B.C.

aced by the tough, uncultured peoples on its borders. These were the Cassites of the Iranian mountains and the Elamites, who lived along the Persian Gulf, awaiting their opportunity for profitable raids.

About 1730 B.C. the Cassites swept down, like the Gutians before them, from the Zagros mountains into the river plains, and by 1600 B.C. were firmly established in Babylon. They were rough, uncivilized hillmen, but shrewd enough to preserve

III-54. Cassite *kudurrus,* or boundary stones. *c.* 1150 B.C.

III-55. Panel of molded bricks, from Susa. *c.* 1150 B.C.

III-56. Silver statuette of worshiper, from Susa. *c.* 1200 B.C.

III-57. Electrum (gold and silver alloy) statuette of worshiper, from Susa. *c.* 1200 B.C.

for bricks but little stone. As we shall see, the technique became more important later. This panel depicts a bull-god with a stylized palm tree and a rather pillar-like goddess, Ninhursag, who lifts her hands in blessing. The figures are well proportioned, and again the old conventions of presenting a figure in relief have been broken. The legs of the bull-god are in profile, but his head as well as his shoulders are seen from the front. The goddess is presented entirely from the front. In metalwork, the Elamite craftsmen attained real mastery; the small statuettes of worshipers carrying animals, entirely Mesopotamian in feeling, have a charm of their own (Plates III-56 and III-57). Under the Cassites and Elamites, the art of what had once been the Babylonian Empire reached its final stage. This was at the period of Egypt's great New Kingdom.

We have seen Mesopotamian civilization develop continuously from the fourth millennium B.C. to the beginning of the first, but by 1200 B.C. this great culture had lost its creative vigor. At this point a Semitic people of immense energy and talent emerged from the city of Ashur in the middle Tigris to become a kingdom, an empire, and a world power. The Assyrians had long been independent, and now they began to extend their frontiers; they dominated the history of Mesopotamia until the fall of Nineveh in 612 B.C. Babylonia was Assyria's chief rival all through this period, and was twice conquered.

The Assyrians were a formidable and gifted people. Warriors, scholars, and artists, utterly fearless, cruel to man and beast, and led by a succession of able and ambitious kings, they respected the past and remained faithful to their own religious traditions.

Although the kings were chosen by the gods, and the land in theory belonged to the patron god, Ashur, the king of Assyria was, in fact, an all-powerful autocrat. His splendid appearance, his rich robes, headdress, and insignia, the court ceremonies, and numerous court officials all exalted his position. He was the first of a long line of oriental despots, the representative and agent of Ashur and the other gods on earth. In Plate III-58 we see a statue of King Ashur-nasir-pal II (883–859), one of the most ruthless conquerors in Mesopotamian history. The sculptor has given the figure a heightened majesty by placing a small head on top of an elongated neck. We feel as if we were standing below the king looking up, and what we see glaring down from above us is a figure of cold cruelty, passionately grasping a symbol of royalty, a weapon he would not hesitate to use. A royal inscription runs: "Ashur and the mighty gods,

III-58. Statue of King Ashur-nasir-pal II of Assyria. Ninth century B.C.

III-59. Statue of the Assyrian god Nabu. Ninth century B.C.

who have made my kingdom great and have given me power and strength, commanded that I should extend the boundaries of their country, and they entrusted to my hand their mighty weapon, the onslaught of battle. Lands, mountains, cities and princes, Ashur's enemies, I have brought under my yoke and subjugated their territories. I fought sixty kings, and established my victorious power over them."

The gods whom the Assyrian kings represented so well were of no more winning aspect than Ashur-nasir-pal himself. In Plate III-59 we see a statue of the god Nabu, protector of scribes and priests, wearing the horned crown of divinity and appearing to sneer through his elaborately curled wig at his worshiper.

The ninth century B.C. is the beginning of the great age of Assyria, when her armies pushed westward opening the way to the rich metal-mining countries of Asia Minor and exacting tribute from weaker states. Ashur-nasir-pal II secured these conquests by ceaseless campaigning and reached the Mediterranean. Under his successors, the kings with names like a roll of war-drums— Tiglath-Pileser, Shalmaneser, Sargon, Sennacherib, Esarhaddon, and Ashurbanipal— the Assyrians conquered Syria, Palestine, and Egypt. They defeated Babylon and forcibly transported conquered peoples from one end of their empire to the other.

By 700 B.C. Assyria ruled from the Nile and the Mediterranean to the Persian Gulf and the Armenian mountains, linking up their empire by efficient communications for trade and the collection of tribute. This spectacular success was due, above all, to the well-organized, well-equipped, and unyielding army of horse-drawn chariots, cavalry, infantry, and archers, usually commanded by the king himself, who rode at the head of

167

his troops. The Assyrians also possessed iron weapons, elaborate siege equipment, and a reputation for savagery unequaled in ancient times. An Assyrian king boasted of flaying his enemies and exhibiting their skins on a wall in which he had entombed them alive.

Great builders of fortresses and especially palaces, the Assyrians also developed the art of relief decoration as never before. Needless to say, the favorite subjects of Assyrian relief sculpture are detailed scenes of military campaigns, victories, and the hunt. Plate III-60 shows a scene from a lion hunt in which two noblemen in a chariot ride down a wounded lion as they bend their bows to shoot another. And now we realize something altogether extraordinary. These people who "delighted in war" were, for some inexplicable reason, great artists. For delicacy and fine workmanship, for accurate portrayal of anatomy and perspective, their reliefs are as fine as anything in the history of Egyptian art; and for sheer power, vitality, and energy, they are greater.

Such reliefs, carved in alabaster, formed a continuous frieze around the walls of the rooms and halls in the splendid palaces built by the kings at Nimrud, Khorsabad, and Nineveh. Human figures were not always successfully portrayed. They were often either rigid and statue-like, as we see Ashurbanipal in Plate III-61, or squat and stiff, like earlier Sumerian figures. This is true

III-60. Scene from a lion hunt, Assyrian. Seventh century B.C.

III-61. Relief of King Ashurbanipal, from Nineveh. Seventh century B.C.

of the seamen unloading tree trunks (Plate III-62) in a relief of a naval expedition bringing cedarwood from Phoenician cities.

But in their animal sculpture, Assyrian artists reveal an intensity of feeling and understanding that appears nowhere else in the entire history of art. The lion hunt carvings from the palace of Ashurbanipal at Nineveh have never been surpassed in their rendering of animals in violent movement (Plates III-63 and III-64). Here, too, we see cruelty—not coarse and brutish, but refined and exquisite—the cruelty of real wounds. One lion, superbly chiseled in the most delicate detail, has been pierced by an arrow through the eye. Another, wounded in the back and with a look of terror in his eyes, stresses every muscle of his powerful forelegs to drag his paralyzed hindquarters. Never before had the struggle against death in man or beast been so dramatically portrayed, and it has rarely been done since. Plate III-65 shows us the free sweep of the hunt. Ashurbanipal and his courtiers and mastiffs are chasing wild asses or horses with bows and arrows. The figures fly freely through the expanse of what must be the open desert, and we can almost feel the speed. On the right, a mare looks back at her foal. If the Assyrians were portrayers of cruelty, they were in a way the finest observers of life in all of ancient art. The artist could not communicate the pride, strength, and agony of wild animals without

III-62. Relief of a naval expedition under Sargon II. Eighth century B.C.

III-63. Relief of a wounded lion, from Nineveh. Seventh century B.C.

III-65. Relief of King Ashurbanipal hunting wild asses or horses, from Nineveh. Seventh century B.C.

III-64. Relief of a wounded lion, from Nineveh. Seventh century B.C.

being moved by them himself. This is the highest achievement in Assyrian art.

The Assyrians shared, too, the Mesopotamian fascination with fantastical creatures, part man and part beast. In the relief from Nimrud (Plate III-66) we see a decorative diety, part human and part bird, picking the fruit of a stylized vine. Winged human forms were a favorite motif, like the little figure in Plate III-67, who is Pazuzu, the demon of sickness. The most important figure, one we see again and again guarding many of the gates and doors of ancient Assyria, is a strange composite creature—a winged bull with human head bearing the horned crown of divinity (Plate III-68). These fantasies, with their great muscular bull torsoes, keen human features, and splendid sweep of arched wing, represented to the Assyrians all that was animal, human, and divine, and, most important, all that was thunderously powerful.

III-66. Relief of a mythical creature, from Nimrud. *c.* 900 B.C.

III-67. Bronze statue of the demon Pazuzu. Ninth century B.C.

In 612 B.C. Nineveh fell to the Assyrian's age-old enemies, the Babylonians, aided by the Medes and Scythians, and with the fall of Nineveh, Assyrian power was destroyed forever. There were few mourners. The biblical prophet Nahum must have spoken for the entire ancient Near East: "There is no healing of thy bruise; thy wound is grievous: all that hear the bruit of thee shall clap the hands over thee: for upon whom hath not thy wickedness passed continuously?"

Babylon, despite its many generations under Cassite rule and its years of subjection to the Assyrians, had never quite lost its great cultural heritage. Now a new dynasty gave the city nearly a century of prosperity in which the arts revived and flourished. Under the Kings Nabopolassar and Nebuchadrezzar the markets of Babylon were thronged with foreign caravans and merchandise, and the city became a center of international trade, the greatest metropolis in the east. It was King Nebuchadrezzar who took the Israelites into captivity, and there is in the Bible an account of the merchandise of Babylon. It is both a fascinating catalog and a great moral judgement:

The merchandise of gold and silver, and precious stones, and of pearls, and fine linen, and purple, and silk, and scarlet, and . . . wood, and all manner of vessels of ivory, and all manner vessels of most precious wood, and of brass, and iron, and marble.

And cinnamon, and odours, and ointments, and frankincense, and wine, and oil, and fine flour, and wheat, and beasts, and sheep, and horses, and chariots, and slaves, and the souls of men.

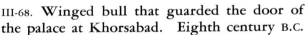

III-68. **Winged bull that guarded the door of the palace at Khorsabad. Eighth century** B.C.

III-69. **The Ishtar Gate in the northern walls of Babylon. Seventh century** B.C.

Temples and ziggurats were rebuilt in the ancient Sumerian cities, and buildings of great magnificence were constructed in Babylon itself. The remains of the great hanging gardens have been found, along with the well that watered its vegetation. Most spectacular was the temple of the city-god Marduk, with its high ziggurat. This was surely the Tower of Babel described in the Bible. The Hebrew captives must have been amazed by the number of languages spoken in the metropolitan city.

Remains of the royal palace were also found, and the tremendous city walls which Herodotus the Greek historian described: a wall 56 miles long, 320 feet high, and wide enough for two chariots to drive over it abreast. The wall had a hundred bronze doors enclosing a city that "exceeded in splendor any city of the known world." These great structures were of mud-brick which has crumbled away so that only shapeless mounds are left, but by carefully sorting the remains brick by brick, arche-

III-70. **A lion in glazed tiles, from the walls of the processional way in Babylon. Seventh century B.C.**

III-71. **A bull in glazed tiles, from the processional way in Babylon. Seventh century B.C.**

ologists have been able to reconstruct many of these monuments on paper, and some in actuality.

A magnificent processional way, paved with alternating red and white stones, led over the river Euphrates on a splendid bridge and through the town to the main temple enclosure, passing through the inner city wall at the Ishtar Gate (Plate III-69). This huge double portal was placed under the protection of Ishtar, the powerful goddess of love and war. The gate has been partly preserved, and although the colored glaze decoration has gone, we can see the outlines of its relief. The crenelated walls flanking the processional way were adorned with glazed brick tiles, and many of these have survived. Huge figures of lions and bulls (which were sacred to Marduk) and dragons were modeled in brilliantly colored relief. Only a few of the many thousands of these figures have survived (Plates III-70 and III-71), but they give us some idea of the effect these splendid beasts must have made, striding along in brilliant earth tones of glazed yellows and whites against a background of deep blue-green.

The walls of Nebuchadrezzar's throne room were decorated with formal flower patterns in the same style. It was this very room in which the last Babylonian king, who was, according to the Bible, Belshar-usur (or Belshazzar), sat feasting and drinking from the vessels stolen from the temple at Jerusalem when

> . . . came forth fingers of a man's hand, and wrote over against the candlestick upon . . . the wall of the king's palace: and the king saw the part of the hand that wrote . . .
>
> And this is the writing that was written, MENE, MENE, TEKEL, UPHARSIN . . . God hath numbered thy kingdom and finished it . . . Thou art weighed in the balances and art found wanting . . . Thy kingdom is divided and given to the Medes and the Persians. . . .

The prophecy was soon fulfilled. Babylon surrendered to King Cyrus in 538 B.C. after a Persian victory near the Tigris. Cyrus was the first of the great Achaemenid Dynasty (550–330 B.C.) to rule Persia. He had already defeated the Medes, whose kingdom was in the north of Iran, and the Lydians under their wealthy king Croesus. But his success in Babylonia began a new era of Persian rule in the Middle East.

The prosperity of Babylon continued for at least another generation, for Cyrus respected the nationality and religion of the peoples he conquered in war. Under this great and magnanimous king and his successors, especially Darius I, Persian rule spread west and south to Egypt and Ethiopia, and east to India. The Persian Empire grew to cover the entire Near and Middle East, to be the largest empire yet known by man, and one of the largest in history.

The center of cultural life in western Asia now shifted from Mesopotamia to Iran. An imperial art and architecture developed, an outward sign of world power. The basic forms followed Mesopotamian traditions, and especially the art of Assyria and Babylonia. How closely Persian sculpture resembled Assyrian we can see if we look at the huge human-headed bulls (Plate III-72) built by King Xerxes at Persepolis, one of the capitals of the Persian empire. These are almost exactly like the human-headed winged bulls of Assyria (Plate III-69). The fragment of a relief from the palace of Darius showing a fight between a lion and a bull (Plate III-73) has the splendid ferocity of the Assyrian animal reliefs. But it has something else, too, and this is another element of Persian art. The Persians inherited from earlier Iranian peoples a great natural gift for decorative design. This decorative interest can be seen in every bit of Persian art—sculptures and reliefs in stone and glazed brick, jewelry and bronze and gold artifacts. The Persians unfailingly combined clarity, precision, and neat, ordered arrangement with invention and a love of splendor, "the old Persian magnificence," as an English traveler in 1628 described it.

Finally, there is a third element in Persian art: the influence of the art just then developing in Greece. In the reign of Darius I, Greek craftsmen were employed at the Persian court, and their influence can be seen in Persian sculpture. Assyrian reliefs are really two-dimensional pictures, the figures merely raised above the background. In

III-72. Human-headed bulls from the gate at Persepolis.   Fifth century B.C.

III-73. Relief of a fight between a lion and a bull, from Persepolis.   Late sixth to early fifth centuries B.C.

the Persian reliefs the figures stand out as three-dimensional forms, a typically Greek approach. The tribute-bearer in Plate III-74 has the beauty of clean lines and proportion which was a Greek ideal. We will notice, too, a greater interest in human anatomy. Moreover, we see in Persian sculpture a new free and sometimes complicated treatment of drapery. In the relief of a tribute-bearer in Plate III-75 we see that the artist has carefully observed how the cloth of the figure's robes would fall if draped in this or that manner, and he has tried to portray this drapery, not as a flat pattern, but with some depth. This is a completely Greek approach.

The most famous palaces built by the Achaemenid rulers were at Susa, the ancient

III-74. Detail from the relief of the tribute-bearers at Persepolis. Late sixth to early fifth centuries B.C.

III-75. Detail from the relief of the tribute-bearers at Persepolis. Late sixth to early fifth centuries B.C.

III-76. Relief of Darius I with his courtiers, from Persepolis. Late sixth to early fifth centuries B.C.

III-77. Part of the ruins of the palace of Darius at Persepolis. Late sixth to early fifth centuries B.C.

capital of Elam, and Persepolis, perhaps the most impressive ruin in the world. Begun by Darius I, it was never entirely completed. Its vast palaces and halls sit on a huge terrace or platform hewn out of the dark gray rock of the mountainside behind it. The terrace was 545 yards long by 330 yards wide, with retaining walls of fitted masonry, some of the blocks weighing 25 tons. Above the stairway an imposing gatehouse led to the main courtyards and the throne room, the Hall of a Hundred Columns begun by Xerxes and finished by his son Artaxerxes I, behind which were the residential palaces.

The relief sculpture was concentrated along the facades of the terraces on which the buildings stood, unlike the Assyrian palace reliefs which adorned the interiors of halls and audience chambers. The Assyrian reliefs were a narrative of actual events, expressively and freely depicted, while the Persian reliefs were an important part of an architectural design. Persian sculpture always centered around the person of the king. The themes were always the same: the king enthroned with the royal bodyguard in attendance, and processions of tribute-bearers from different countries. The relief of Darius I with his courtiers in Plate III-76, and the procession of figures in Plate III-77 are excellent examples. Such designs, with the formal repetition of figures, were perfect compliments to architectural forms. In Plate III-78 we see a frieze of delegates from vassal countries bearing tribute. The figures wear long tunics and loose trousers, and they lead a completely

III-78. Frieze from the staircase leading to the king's audience chamber at Persepolis. Late sixth to early fifth centuries B.C.

III-79. One of the Imperial bodyguard from a procession in glazed ceramic, from the palace of Darius at Susa. Early fifth century B.C.

realistic camel, waddling along on floppy legs.

Persian reliefs were originally brilliant with color; turquoise and blue, scarlet and green, purple and yellow have all left traces on the stone. At Susa, which the Achaemenid kings rebuilt as their capital, panels of glazed brick were used instead of stone for the royal palace. This Babylonian technique of decorating walls was adopted, and figures of animals were sharply modeled in relief on tiles. These were dispersed on a textile-like background enriched with stylized plant and flower designs, each brick a subtly different shade of color. The most famous frieze has an entirely Persian theme. It represents the royal bodyguard, the Ten Thousand, so called because their strength was always made up to that number. In Plate III-79 we see one of the Imperial bodyguard, and here we notice, in the ornamentation of the realistically folded drapery, the intricate and rich decoration always thought of as Persian.

Persian architects, who often came from the Greek cities of the Empire, seem to have been fascinated by columns. The throne rooms and audience halls at Persepolis and Susa had innumerable ornamental pillars supporting roofs of cedar and silver, with silver rings for colored hangings. There is a vivid and detailed description of the palace of Xerxes (Ahasuerus) at Susa (Shushan) in the First Book of Esther in the Old Testament. The details and moldings of Persian columns resemble those of the Ionic columns in Greek cities of the Aegean coast, which formed part of the Persian empire. But one feature was original: the capitals or impost blocks for carrying beams, were sculpted in the form of the foreparts of two kneeling animals, bulls or dragons. These animal capitals are extremely decorative, and

III-80. **Marble bull capital, from the palace of Darius at Susa. Early fifth century B.C.**

179

III-81. Silver ritual vase, Persian.

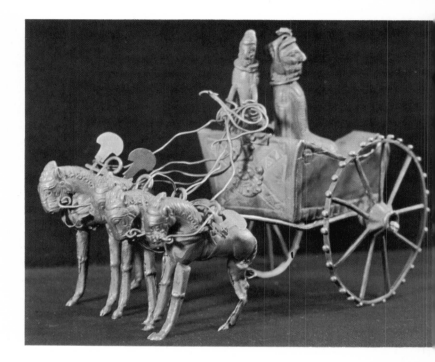

III-82. Gold chariot drawn by four horses, part of the Oxus Treasure. Sixth to fourth centuries B.C.

III-83. Gold bracelet from the Oxus Treasure. Sixth to fourth centuries B.C.

they show a perfect collaboration between architect and sculptor. The majestic bull from the palace of Artaxerxes at Susa is such a capital (Plate III-80). The effect of a ceiling supported by these superb and powerful beasts can be imagined.

Persia was famous for her wealth, and the work of her goldsmiths and silversmiths was intricate and charming. The silver ritual vase (Plate III-81), with its base in the form of a wild goat, is particularly lovely. The Iranian plateau is the home of these agile, slender creatures, which often inspired Persian craftsmen. Many such objects were found in the Oxus Treasure, a collection containing much Persian goldsmiths' work, discovered in the last century near the river of Amu Darya, the ancient Oxus. These pieces may have come from the treasury of some unknown temple in what is now Uzbekistan. Among them is a little gold chariot drawn by four horses (Plate III-82), and a splendid gold bracelet, originally inlaid with precious stones, in which are represented two winged beasts facing each other, another favorite Persian motif (Plate III-83).

It happened that on the edge of the Persian empire, on the coast of Anatolia opposite Greece, there lived colonies of Ionian Greeks. In 499 B.C. these colonies rebelled against the rule of the great Darius I and sacked Sardes with the aid of allies from the Greek mainland. Darius realized that if he were to hold the Ionian Greek cities within his own territory, he would have to deal a death blow to the mainland Greeks. This small and seemingly barbarous people could not have looked like difficult opponents to the Emperor of all the East, but when he descended on Greece with a large army, he was defeated at Marathon. Darius did not know it, but he was facing men of a new type, free men ruled by laws of their own making. A Greek adviser later tried to explain his countrymen to the Persian court, which was accustomed to rule by the will of one man: ". . . fighting together they are the best soldiers in the world. They are free—yes—but not entirely free; for they have a master, and that master is Law, which they fear much more than your subjects fear you. Whatever that master commands, they do; and his command never varies; it is never to retreat in battle, however great the odds, but always to stand firm, and to conquer or die."

Darius died with Greece still undefeated, and his successor Xerxes set about mounting against the small, independent states of Greece the greatest military expedition man had yet experienced. There is disagreement about the size of the Persian forces, but Herodotus puts the number at no less than five million in all. The great army crossed the Hellespont on two bridges made of ships lashed together, and it took all of seven days for the troops to cross, traveling at a steady pace. Marching with the Persians were many peoples of the ancient Near East: Egyptians, Libyans, Nubians, Assyrians, all those who were accustomed to following a god-chosen king back and forth across the map of the Near East to victory after victory. To one observer, it looked as if the whole world were marching on Greece, and so it was. The whole of the ancient civilization of the Near East was attacking the new peoples of Europe, their civilization still young, their institutions so different and untried.

The Greek city states united as best they could, and with a courage next to madness a group of perhaps six thousand, led by the men of Athens and Sparta, prepared to meet the five million at the narrow pass of Thermopylae. The Greeks were extraordinarily successful and slaughtered battalion after battalion of the invaders, but a secret route was disclosed to the Persians, and when they realized they were outflanked, most of the Greeks retreated. To the Spartans, though, retreat was unknown, and so their contingent of three hundred remained to stave off the millions with their lances, their swords, and their bare hands. On their grave was written, "Traveler, tell those at Sparta that here we lie, faithful to their command."

The Persian army now descended on Attica, there to be met not only by the courage of the free men of Athens and her allies, but by the wisdom of one of the greatest leaders of men in history, Themistocles. Themistocles possessed what the Greeks call *pronoia,* foresight of a very high degree. The oracle at Delphi had predicted that Athens would be saved by "wooden walls." Themistocles had taken "wooden walls" to mean ships, and when the city had enjoyed a sudden windfall of wealth, he had counseled the Athenians to build a powerful navy.

The Persians marched into the city of Athens with ease and burned it to the ground, making way, although they little knew it, for its rebirth as the greatest monument in the history of art. Meanwhile, the Athenians had retreated to the offshore island of Salamis, where they awaited the enemy with their navy. The Persian fleet was tricked into joining battle in the narrow straights of Salamis, where their greater speed and numbers were of no use, and it was totally destroyed. Athens and her allies were victorious, and the great army of Xerxes was obliged to find its way back to Asia as best it could. The Persian Empire was not destroyed; it was not even fatally weakened. But on that day, September 28, 480 B.C., something far more important had happened—the torch of that thing we call civilization was seized by Europeans from the hands of the ancient peoples of the Near East.

# LIST OF ILLUSTRATIONS

II-27. Relief from the tomb of Akhty-hotpe near Sakkareh, showing servants bringing geese and ducks. *c.* 2500 B.C. The Louvre, Paris.

II-28. Relief from the tomb of Merer-wy-kuy near Sakkareh, showing Merer-wy-kuy standing in a boat. *c.* 2400 B.C.

II-29. Relief from the tomb of Merer-wy-kuy near Sakkareh, showing fishermen. *c.* 2400 B.C.

II-30. Painting of geese, from the tomb of Itet at Meidum. 2700 B.C. Cairo Museum.

II-31. Green basalt relief statue of King Mycerinus. Fourth Dynasty. Cairo Museum.

II-32. Basalt statue of Princess Redyzet. Third Dynasty. Egyptian Museum, Turin.

II-33. Limestone statue of King Djoser. Third Dynasty. Cairo Museum.

II-34. Diorite statue of King Chephren. Fourth Dynasty. Cairo Museum.

II-35. Head of King Radedef. Fourth Dynasty. The Louvre, Paris.

II-36. Alabaster head of King Mycerinus. Fourth Dynasty. Cairo Museum.

II-37. Granite head of King Woser-kuf. Fifth Dynasty. Cairo Museum.

II-38. Copper statue of King Pepy I. Sixth Dynasty. Cairo Museum.

II-39. Limestone statue of Ti. Fifth Dynasty. Cairo Museum.

II-40. Limestone statues of Prince Re-hotep and his wife Nefret. Fourth Dynasty. Cairo Museum.

II-41. Statue of Re-hotep (detail). Fourth Dynasty. Cairo Museum.

II-42. Statue of Nefret (detail). Fourth Dynasty. Cairo Museum.

II-43. Limestone statue of a scribe. Fifth Dynasty. The Louvre, Paris.

II-44. Limestone statue of a scribe. Fifth Dynasty. Cairo Museum.

II-45. Head of the statue of Ranofer. Fifth Dynasty. Cairo Museum.

II-46. "Sheikh el beled." Fifth Dynasty. The Louvre, Paris.

II-47. Wooden statue of an official of Memphis and his wife. Fifth Dynasty. The Louvre, Paris.

II-48. The dwarf Seneb and his family. Sixth Dynasty. Cairo Museum.

II-49. Funerary stele of King Wadji-Djet. First Dynasty. The Louvre, Paris.

II-50. The sarcophagus of Rawer. Old Kingdom. Cairo Museum.

II-51. Entrance to the mastabeh of Ti, near Sakkareh. Fifth Dynasty.

II-52. The Step Pyramid of Djoser at Sakkareh. *c.* 2800 B.C.

II-53. The enclosing wall and Step Pyramid at Sakkareh. *c.* 2800 B.C.

II-54. Porch of the Hall of the Columns at Sakkareh. *c.* 2800 B.C.

II-55. Hall of the Columns at Sakkareh. *c.* 2800 B.C.

II-56. Pyramid of Snefru at Medum. *c.* 2700 B.C.

II-57. The pyramids of Cheops, Chephren, and Mycerinus at Gizeh. 2700–2600 B.C.

II-58. The Great Pyramid of Cheops at Gizeh. 2700–2600 B.C.

II-59. The sphinx at Gizeh. *c.* 2700 B.C.

II-60. The sphinx at Gizeh. *c.* 2700 B.C.

II-61. Limestone statue of King Montu-hotpe II. *c.* 2050 B.C. Cairo Museum.

II-62. Granite head of King Amun-em-het I. *c.* 2000 B.C. British Museum, London.

II-63. Sphinx of Amun-em-het III. Middle Kingdom. Cairo Museum.

II-64. Statue of Sesostris III. *c.* 1850 B.C. Cairo Museum.

II-65. Wooden statue of Nakhty. *c.* 2000 B.C. The Louvre, Paris.

II-66. Relief of Sesostris I and the god Ptah from the pavilion of Sesostris at Karnak. *c.* 2000 B.C. Cairo Museum.

II-67. Relief of Sesostris I and the god Amun from the pavilion of Sesostris at Karnak. *c.* 2000 B.C. Cairo Museum.

II-68. The *ka* of King Hor. Nineteenth century B.C. Cairo Museum.

II-69. Statuette of a servant girl. *c.* 2000 B.C. The Louvre, Paris.

II-70. Model of a peasant guiding a plow. Middle Kingdom. British Museum, London.

II-71. Model boat of painted wood. Middle Kingdom. The Louvre, Paris.

II-72. Blue ceramic hippopotamus. Middle Kingdom. The Louvre, Paris.

II-73. Crowned head of Amun-em-het III. Middle Kingdom. Cairo Museum.

II-74. Funerary temple of Queen Hat-shepsut at Deir el Bahri. Eighteenth Dynasty.

II-75. Square pillars from the chapel of Hat-Hor in the temple of Queen Hat-shepsut at Deir el Bahri. Eighteenth Dynasty.

II-76. Relief of Queen Hat-shepsut drinking from the udder of the Cow-goddess Hat-Hor, from Deir el Bahri. Eighteenth Dynasty.

II-77. The temple of Amun at Karnak. New Kingdom.

II-78. Lotus columns from the temple of Amun at Luxor. New Kingdom.

II-79. Avenue of limestone rams leading to temple of Amun at Karnak. New Kingdom.

II-80. The courtyard of Ramesses II of the temple of Amun at Luxor, with a statue of the god protecting the king. Nineteenth Dynasty.

II-81. Statues between the columns of the courtyard of Ramesses II of the temple of Amun at Luxor. Nineteenth Dynasty.

II-82. The Colossi of Memnon. Eighteenth Dynasty.

II-83. Statuette in white marble of Thut-mose III. Eighteenth Dynasty. Cairo Museum.

II-84. Statue in red granite of Amun-hotpe II. Eighteenth Dynasty. Egyptian Museum, Turin.

II-85. Statue of a young scribe. Fourteenth century B.C. Ny Carlsberg Glyptotek, Copenhagen.

II-86. The sphinx at Memphis. 1600–1500 B.C.

II-87. Granite group of Thut-mose IV and his mother. Eighteenth Dynasty. Cairo Museum.

II-88. Painted relief from the funerary chapel of Thut-mose III. Eighteenth Dynasty. Cairo Museum.

II-89. Interior of the funerary chapel of Thut-mose III. Eighteenth Dynasty. Cairo Museum.

II-90. Detail of a wall painting from the funerary chapel of Thut-mose III. Eighteenth Dynasty. Cairo Museum.

II-91. Wall painting of a group of ladies at a party, from the tomb of Neb-Amun. Fifteenth century B.C. British Museum, London.

II-92. Wall painting of slave girls dancing, from the tomb of Neb-Amun. Fifteenth century B.C. British Museum, London.

II-93. Wall painting of a view of Neb-Amun's garden, from the tomb of Neb-Amun. Fifteenth century B.C. British Museum, London.

II-94. Wall painting of Neb-Amun hunting in the marshes, from the tomb of Neb-Amun. Fifteenth century B.C. British Museum, London.

II-95. Limestone group of Amun-hotpe IV (Akh-en-Aten) and his wife Nefret-ity. Fourteenth century B.C. The Louvre, Paris.

II-96. Wall painting of two of the daughters of Akh-en-Aten from Tell el Amarneh. Fourteenth century B.C. Ashmolean Museum, Oxford.

II-97. Fragment of a relief showing Akh-en-Aten, Nefret-ity, and a daughter raising offerings to Aten, from Tell el Amarneh. Fourteenth century B.C. Cairo Museum.

II-98. Wooden head from Tell el Amarneh, probably part of the decoration of a harp. Fourteenth century B.C. The Louvre, Paris.

II-99. Head of Queen Nefret-ity, from Tell el Amarneh. Fourteenth century B.C. Former State Museum, Berlin.

II-100. Quarzite head of Queen Nefret-ity, from Tell el Amarneh. Fourteenth century B.C. Cairo Museum.

II-101. Statuette in red quartz, probably of Nefret-ity. Fourteenth century B.C. The Louvre, Paris.

II-102. Relief statue of a lady, the wife of general Nakht-Min. Fourteenth century B.C. Cairo Museum.

II-103. Middle coffin of King Tut-ankh-Amun. Eighteenth Dynasty. Cairo Museum.

II-104. Gold base of the middle coffin of King Tut-ankh-Amun. Eighteenth Dynasty. Cairo Museum.

II-105. Detail of the inner coffin of King Tut-ankh-Amun. Eighteenth Dynasty. Cairo Museum.

II-106. Gold mask of King Tut-ankh-Amun. Eighteenth Dynasty. Cairo Museum.

II-107. Gold statuettes of the goddess Sakhmet and the god Ptah, from the tomb of Tut-ankh-Amun. Eighteenth Dynasty. Cairo Museum.

II-108. Shrine of gilded wood from the tomb of Tut-ankh-Amun. Eighteenth Dynasty. Cairo Museum.

III-40. Standing statue of Gudea of Lagash. *c.* 2200 B.C. Ny Carlsberg Glyptotek, Copenhagen.

III-41. Statue of a woman wearing a kerchief and necklace, from Lagash. *c.* 2200 B.C. The Louvre, Paris.

III-42. Statue or Ur-Ningirsu of Lagash. Twenty-second century B.C. The Louvre, Paris.

III-43. Diorite head of a young man, probably Ur-Ningursu of Lagash. Twenty-second century B.C. The Louvre, Paris.

III-44. The Code of Hammurabi, found at Susa. Eighteenth century B.C. The Louvre, Paris.

III-45. Statue of Ishtup-Ilum, governor of Mari. *c.* 1900 B.C.(?) Aleppo Museum, Syria.

III-46. A man in a tasseled cloak, found at Mari. *c.* 1900 B.C.(?) Aleppo Museum, Syria.

III-47. Goddess with a flowing vase, from Mari. *c.* 1800 B.C. Aleppo Museum, Syria.

III-48. Statue of Idi-Ilum, prince of Mari. *c.* 1900 B.C.(?) The Louvre, Paris.

III-49. Detail of mural painting, from the palace of Mari. *c.* 1800 B.C. Aleppo Museum, Syria.

III-50. Detail of mural painting, from the palace of Mari. *c.* 1800 B.C. Aleppo Museum, Syria.

III-51. Bronze head of a lion, from Mari. *c.* 1950 B.C. Aleppo Museum, Syria.

III-52. Bronze group of three ibexes, from Larsa. 1900–1800 B.C. The Louvre, Paris.

III-53. Terra-cotta mold, from Mari. *c.* 1800 B.C. Aleppo Museum, Syria.

III-54. Cassite *kudurrus,* or boundary stones. *c.* 1150 B.C. *A* and *C,* The Louvre, Paris; *B,* British Museum, London.

III-55. Panel of molded bricks, from Susa. *c.* 1150 B.C. The Louvre, Paris.

III-56. Silver statuette of worshiper, from Susa. *c.* 1200 B.C. The Louvre, Paris.

III-57. Electrum (gold and silver alloy) statuette of worshiper, from Susa. *c.* 1200 B.C. The Louvre, Paris.

III-58. Statue of King Ashur-nasir-pal II of Assyria. Ninth century B.C. British Museum, London.

III-59. Statue of the Assyrian god Nabu. Ninth century B.C. British Museum, London.

III-60. Scene from a lion hunt, Assyrian. Seventh century B.C. British Museum, London.

III-61. Relief of King Ashurbanipal, from Nineveh. Seventh century B.C. The Louvre, Paris.

III-62. Relief of a naval expedition under Sargon II. Eighth century B.C. The Louvre, Paris.

III-63. Relief of a wounded lion, from Nineveh. Seventh century B.C. British Museum, London.

III-64. Relief of a wounded lion, from Nineveh. Seventh century B.C. British Museum, London.

III-65. Relief of King Ashurbanipal hunting wild asses or horses, from Nineveh. Seventh century B.C. British Museum, London.

III-66. Relief of a mythical creature, from Nimrud. *c.* 900 B.C. British Museum, London.

III-67. Bronze statue of the demon Pazuzu. Ninth century B.C. The Louvre, Paris.

III-68. Winged bull that guarded the door of the palace at Khorsabad. Eighth century B.C. The Louvre, Paris.

III-69. The Ishtar Gate in the northern walls of Babylon. Seventh century B.C.

III-70. A lion in glazed tiles, from the walls of the processional way in Babylon. Seventh century B.C. Ny Carlsberg Glyptotek, Copenhagen.

III-71. A bull in glazed tiles, from the processional way in Babylon. Seventh century B.C. Ny Carlsberg Glyptotek, Copenhagen.

III-72. Human-headed bulls from the gate at Persepolis. Fifth century B.C.

III-73. Relief of a fight between a lion and a bull, from Persepolis. Late sixth to early fifth centuries B.C.

III-74. Detail from the relief of the tribute-bearers at Persepolis. Late sixth to early fifth centuries B.C. British Museum, London.

III-75. Detail from the relief of the tribute-bearers at Persepolis. Late sixth to early fifth centuries B.C. Ny Carlsberg Glyptotek, Copenhagen.

III-76. Relief of Darius I with his courtiers, from Persepolis. Late sixth to early fifth centuries B.C.

III-77. Part of the ruins of the palace of Darius at Persepolis. Late sixth to early fifth centuries B.C.

III-78. Frieze from the staircase leading to the king's audience chamber at Persepolis. Late sixth to early fifth centuries B.C.

III-79. One of the Imperial bodyguard from a procession in glazed ceramic, from the palace of Darius at Susa. Early fifth century B.C. British Museum, London.

III-80. Marble bull capital, from the palace of Darius at Susa. Early fifth century B.C. The Louvre, Paris.

III-81. Silver ritual vase, Persian. The Louvre, Paris.

III-82. Gold chariot drawn by four horses, part of the Oxus Treasure. Sixth to fourth centuries B.C. The Louvre, Paris.

III-83. Gold bracelet from the Oxus Treasure. Sixth to fourth centuries B.C. British Museum, London.

# INDEX